MW00887320

La Santisima Muerte

A Guide for the Three-Robed System

Steven Bragg
Copyright 2020

This photo and cover photo by Steven Bragg

This is a collection of articles, lore, devotional instruction, prayers, and workings for the Santisima Muerte within a three-robed system, as it has been practiced by Steven Bragg, founder of the New Orleans Chapel of the Santisima Muerte, who received his teachings from Nicholas Arnoldi, who received his teachings from "Don Gilberto" of an area south of Tijuana, Mexico, in 2001.

Much of the instructional information was included in two previous booklets, *La Santisima Muerte: Devotional Guide of the Most Holy Death*, and *La Santisima Muerte: Working With Her Robes,* released in 2016. Combined into one volume, several other articles and prayers have been added to this version, spanning the years of 2011 to 2019, and an expanded article on ancestors first written in 2002.

Over the last decade or so, devotion to La Santa Muerte has developed dramatically, especially outside of La Muerte's home country of Mexico. As the author of this work, I recognize all forms and systems of her devotion to be valid, given that it is done with love and respect from the point of view of the practitioner. However a person feels pulled to honor and work with La Milagrosa is the way each person should go. This work, though, focuses on one system steeped in folk Catholicism, employing only the white, red, and black robes of La Muerte. My hope is that this will at the very least enhance the reader's understanding and devotion in some small way.

May La Santisima Muerte bless all who read this.

Table of Contents

Articles
Who Is La Santisima Muerte?....................................5
An Updated Introduction to La Santisima
Muerte……………………………………………….13
Is La Santisima Muerte an Aztec Goddess?.............17
What to Call Devotees and Workers of La Santa
Muerte…………………………………………...……..20

Lore and Instructions
The Three Robes………………………………………22
Lore and Guidelines……………………………..28
Preparing the Altar…………………………………31
Setting Up an Altar for La Santisima Muerte…….37
Offerings………………………………………44
Objects, Symbols, and Acts of Devotion…………..48
Working with La Santisima Muerte……………….54

Prayers
Opening and Ending Prayers………………………65
Devotional Prayers for the Three Robes…………..69
Chaplet of the Santisima Muerte…………………..71
Various Prayers, Invocations, and Novenas………77

Additional Information
The Ancestors…………………………………………92
A Few Cemetery Guidelines……………………….99
Origin of the New Orleans Chapel of the   Santisima
Muerte………………………………………………...106
Liturgical Calendar for the New Orleans Chapel of
the Santisima Muerte…………………………….108

Who Is La Santisima Muerte?
Written in 2012

La Flaka (the Skinny Lady), La Huesuda (the Boney Lady), La Niña (the Girl), La Madrina (the Godmother), Santa Muerte ("Saint" Death)...these are all names given to a very powerful and popular folk saint from Mexico, La Santisima Muerte (the Most Holy Death). Santisima Muerte is a complex figure, having taken on Her most recent manifestation through the same Catholic land that provided the world with what is believed to be the most widely venerated face of the Virgin Mary, Our Lady of Guadalupe. Although She is denounced by the Catholic priests and bishops as a figure of Satanic worship, Santisima Muerte's popularity over the last decade has exploded. From an estimated 500,000 devotees ten years ago to possibly over 12 million today, it seems that Lady Death is wasting no time in making known Her presence and power among the living. Her devotion has now bled across Mexico's borders into many other Latin American countries, as well as into the U.S. Many chapels and a few churches have been established in several places where Mexican immigrants have settled, but these visible establishments are in no way indicative of the number of private altars and shrines most keep in their homes, secretly in many cases.

So, what lies behind this exponential growth of an enigmatic, borderline occult figure, bearing the stark image of the European Grim Reaper, complete with skeleton, cloak, and scythe? What is the appeal of a constant reminder of our own mortality and inevitable death? Despite being labeled a "Narco Saint," whose tattoos give law enforcement officers reason to detain and discriminate, Santisima Muerte refuses to allow any establishment, including the Catholic Church, to slow the growth of Her devotion or sway the minds of those for whom She has performed miracles. In this article, I'd like to share my own personal beliefs about Santisima Muerte, stemming from the teaching I received from a person who lived in Mexico and studied under an hechicero (sorcerer), as well as my own experiences with La Milagrosa (the Miraculous One). My hope is to provide those interested with a bit of information about Santisima Muerte and to help dispel much of the misinformation, causing La Santisima to be feared and demonized by Her many detractors.

I recommend the following: *La Santisima Muerte – A Mexican Folk Saint*, by E. Bryant Holman; *Devoted to Death – Santa Muerte, the Skeleton Saint*, by Prof. R. Andrew Chestnut; and the 2008 DVD documentary, *La Santa Muerte – Saint Death*, directed by Eva Aridjis (with English subtitles).

In the Beginning, God Created...

Exactly from where the current figure of La Santisima Muerte originated is very hard to say. There are theories that She is the revival of the pre-Hispanic Mexican goddess of death, Mitchecacihuatl, that She may be a re-invention of the female Grim Reaper from Spain, La Parca, that She was once a Mexican Catholic nun, and that She came from Italy with roots going all the way back to the Fates of ancient Greece. Regardless of all this, Santisima Muerte now presents Herself as the embodiment of Death itself, with power over the living unrivaled by any other saint, spirit, or deity. However, there is one catch. She chose to manifest through a Catholic culture, and Catholic is how She sees Herself.

6

The Catholic/Christian creation story has been tweaked to include Her, for as Adam and Eve ate of the forbidden fruit in the Garden of Eden, Death entered the world as an active force. Santisima is also given credit for being the Angel of Death who reaped the first-born sons of Egypt in the Book of Exodus. However, Her most proud moment was when God ordered Santisima to reap His only Son, Jesus, and therefore Good Friday is Her most holy feast day, a close second being the Halloween/All Saints Day/All Souls Day celebrations.

La Muerte has usurped the position of a few traditional Catholic figures, such as St. Michael the Archangel, in standing and power. She is considered to be "second in command" after God, for whatever God creates, Santisima takes away. However, She hasn't given the pink slip to the well-known warrior saint like She has to a few others, such as St. Jude. Although Santisima requires Her own space, She does allow two figures of Catholic Mexico to remain close to Her. St. Michael guards and protects Her altars, statues, and devotees from dark forces, while Guadalupe is said to be Her sister or Her "light half."

Although Death is present the world over, and many religions and spiritual traditions have their own images and names for it, when calling upon Death as La Santisima Muerte, it is through the Catholic prayers, always asking God's permission to invoke Her, that She works the best and responds to prayers. Removing her from this paradigm is something I strongly advise against. For those who are uncomfortable with the Catholic aspects, think of it as being respectful to a very powerful force. You don't have to be Catholic yourself to pray to or work with Her, although the vast majority of Her devotees in Mexico consider themselves

Catholics. I also advise against placing Santisima into the hierarchy of other spiritual systems, such as Neo-Pagan traditions and the Afro-Caribbean traditions, i.e. Santeria, Vodou, and Palo. She is a very proud spiritual being who enjoys Her own services and altar spaces, and no matter how much a person believes he or she knows about different spiritual systems and how they work, Santisima will always know more.

...A Holy Trinity...

Although I recognize that there are other ways of working with Santisima Muerte and see where many others in Mexico have her wearing different colored robes, the way She came to me, and the way in which I was taught, was through a tri-colored system. For me, Santisima wears only three robes: white, red, and black. When She wears the white robe, She is La Blanca (the White). She is called La Roja (the Red) while wearing her crimson cloak, and She is La Negra (the Black) when She wraps around Her the shadows of the night. Each cloak alters Her personality, and therefore, She is approached differently according to the color of Her robe. However, like Her masculine counterpart, the Father, Son, and Holy Spirit, Santisima is three persons in one, a feminine Holy Trinity.

La Blanca is the eldest and purest of the three. She sits at the right hand of God, and She is the one most devotees begin with. Peace, healing, cleansing and purifying are all within Her domain. Her highest blessing is the death of old age and a content heart. Her purity is such that it must be protected by covering Her statue when one has any major dealings with La Negra.

La Roja is the robe associated with worldly matters. Money, love, sex, the courts, business, and justice all fall within Her domain. She is a most accomplished love sorceress, and is famous for bringing back wandering lovers and husbands, especially when there are children involved. However, She is equally skilled at manipulating court systems in favor of Her devotees. The type of death La Roja is associated with tends to involve a bodily fluid the same color as Her robe.

La Negra, though, is the hottest and most dangerous robe of La Santisima. She can protect against the darkest forces, spirits, and witchcraft; even the demons of Hell fear Her. But just as She can protect against them, She can also send them. This is where we are reminded that Death stands outside of our human systems of ethics and morality. Although it's believed that Santisima only reaps at the order of God, I sometimes wonder if La Negra may sometimes use Her powers of persuasion to gain the consent of the Divine Almighty, or simply take matters into her own hands, in certain cases involving the wishes of Her most devout devotees. Diseases are considered to be among La Negra's children, and these are the majority of the deaths given over to Her.

It is within this complete system of La Blanca, La Roja, and La Negra that a spiritual worker dedicated to Santisima Muerte can petition La Muerte for any problem a person may have. The media-driven reputation She has for only being honored by drug dealers and criminals is but a fraction of the services She has to offer. The majority of Her devotees who know the three-colored path focus mainly on La Blanca and La Roja, leaving La Negra to the more experienced spiritual workers.

...To Help the People.

Traditionally there are two levels of dealing with La Huesuda. The first and most general is that of the devotee. Santisima will receive offerings and prayers from anyone. Using Her own system of justice, She will weigh each prayer in Her scales and decide for Herself if She will grant the request. For most people She will perform miracles from time to time, however She does expect life-long devotion after that. But Death gets everyone in the end, either way it goes, and it's because of this that She does not discriminate and accepts everyone. Whereas the Catholic Church will turn its back on homosexuals, criminals, those on the fringes of society, La Madrina welcomes them all with open arms.

The other level is that of spiritual worker. In Mexico, there are three general areas of spiritual workers, but the lines between these blur quite a bit, so it's difficult to categorize every individual and his or her practices. Curanderos (male) and curanderas (female) tend to focus on healing and doing what would be considered "right hand" spiritual work. Hechiceros(as) tend to draw more from Native practices and can, as they say, work with both hands. Brujos(as) are generally thought to be more adept with darker workings, those of the so-called left-hand path. Any of these can and do incorporate Santisima Muerte into their workings, as She is thought to have knowledge of all magical and spiritual systems, though She tends to think more highly of some than of others.

Presently, there are many from outside of Mexico and its traditional systems who Santisima is calling upon to work with her. And rest assured, Santisima chooses the worker, not the other way around. A person can receive all the training associated with Her, but if She rejects the person there is nothing to be done about it. Among those She does choose I've noticed several similarities, such as an intimate knowledge of how to work with the dead and the dangers associated with venturing into her home, the cemetery. She very much loves and protects those within her home, and She appreciates it when Her workers honor their own ancestors. There also tends to be a working knowledge of a system similar to Afro-Caribbean spiritual practices, the hoodoo of the Southern U.S., and traditional folk magic in general. Also, She tends to work better and faster for those who treat Her like a Catholic saint and observe certain guidelines.

In the End, La Muerte

Far from being the Satanic symbol of cartels and criminal activity, Santisima Muerte came into my life with a force so powerful and beautiful that it redefined many of my previous spiritual beliefs. Being touched by this Heavenly Power brings with it a new understanding of Death, its place within the cycle of Life, and renews the appreciation I have for each day I'm given. She is a mother, a sister, a protector, a healer, and so much more. Her devotion continues to grow every day, as She turns no one away.

Death, as La Santisima Muerte, is rising to a much higher place than it's been in recent history. Why this is happening remains to be seen. Perhaps this is due to the current state of our Western societies. Perhaps it's due to some larger phase in human existence for which we are on the threshold. Most likely, those of us alive today may not know until we are finally embraced by Her boney arms and given Her eternal kiss.

11

An altar by the author, photo by Steven Bragg

An Updated Introduction to La Santisima Muerte
Written in 2019

Devotion to La Santa Muerte (Spanish for Saint Death or Holy Death) is one of the fastest growing spiritual phenomena in the Western Hemisphere. According to Dr. Andrew Chesnut the estimated number of followers went from around five million in 2009 to about ten to twelve million in 2018, and this number continues to rise as her reputation spreads beyond the borders of her Mexican homeland. She's also known as La Santísima Muerte (the Most Holy Death,) La Huesuda (the Bony One), La Niña Blanca (the White Little Girl,) La Milagrosa (the Miraculous One,) and many other names. She has the reputation for quickly working miracles and not turning anyone away, which has contributed to her explosive popularity within marginalized communities. Despite constant attacks by representatives of the Catholic Church, Santa Muerte's devotion as a folk saint has grown to rival popular traditional saints, such as Saint Michael and Saint Jude. Chesnut refers to this growth as "meteoric," and it shows no sign of slowing down.

Santa Muerte appears as a skeleton robed in a wide variety of colors, holding different objects associated with death. Sometimes she looks more like the European Grim Reaper, while at other times she resembles modernized Central American underworld deities of pre-colonial cultures. However, even though she is seen as a personification of death, her devotees approach her with all manner of requests, ranging from love to healing to money to anything else they may need. For many people living in poverty-stricken and dangerous conditions, praying to the guardian between life and death sometimes seems like their only option, but even for others she's known to work just as fast and with just as much force.

It was in the poor neighborhoods of Mexico City where the Bony Lady began to enjoy her current rise to fame. Professor Chesnut, in his book "Devoted to Death," provides a detailed account of the documented history of the folk saint, but in summary the first public shrine to Santa Muerte was established by Doña Romero Romero in the rough neighborhood of Tepito in 2001. Before this there is little documentation of her existence beyond an early Inquisitional record in the 1700s and anthropological studies beginning in the mid-1900s. Of course, as a folk practice, oral lore and family stories are plentiful as to her origins and practices, but rarely do they agree on where she came from or how she became what she is now. From 2001 onward there have been many more public shrines erected in her honor and several churches and organizations established promoting and spreading her devotion.

As for her origin, one of the most probable theories is the one Chesnut proposes in Devoted to Death. He suggests that as the Spanish colonized what became Mexico, they brought with them the image and concept of La Parca, a female grim reaper who collects the souls of the dead and takes them to where they need to go. Because of the Black Plague during the Middle Ages death became personified all over Europe in various ways. La Parca most likely merged with the remnants of the various underworld and death deities of pre-Christian Central American religions and eventually emerged as La Santa Muerte, remaining in the shadows and developing in slightly different ways in the various

14

regions of Mexico. It's probable that as her devotion began to spread in the different areas it merged with whatever folk magico-religious systems it encountered. This would account for some of the older varying systems that emerged prior to the more recent practices of the last few years where a good bit of New Age and Western Occult practices have appeared, mainly from non-Latino sources.

Early on Santa Muerte's devotion spread south into the spiritually similar cultures of other Central American countries and into the border states of the U.S. following her devotees as they immigrated north. According to several personal accounts Guatemala's All Saints Day and All Souls Day celebrations have included her for many years in their cemetery services, while she's been seen in many locations of southern California and Texas for well over a decade. Candles bearing her image are now found in stores in almost all the continental U.S. states. Due to the internet and world-wide shipping her images, statues, and products are beginning to appear all over the world.

About a decade after the establishment of her first public shrine in Mexico, Holy Death began crossing into non-Hispanic communities in the U.S. In northern California a woman of Danish descent created the Santisima Muerte Chapel of Perpetual Pilgrimage. In 2012 I founded the New Orleans Chapel of the Santisima Muerte in New Orleans, LA, and I passed it to a local botanica in 2018 before relocating to Chicago, IL. Other non-Latino churches and organizations have been created since in various locations in the U.S.

Spiritual merchandizing companies and botánicas (stores that sell spiritual supplies) have also played a large role in the spread and development of Santa Muerte's devotional practices. One of the earliest accounts of the mid-1900s shows a simple image of the folk saint wearing a red robe and being prayed to in order to bring back errant lovers and husbands. Today, because of the merchandizing effects, her images include a dizzying array of colors, postures, objects, and charms for all sorts of purposes. She can be found standing, enthroned, atop a globe or mound of skulls or pile of money, as winged, astride a horse, and all of these can be found in almost any color including multi-colors, as well as garbed in gold or paper money. Any of these may also include magical charms attached to the image, such as mirrors, evil eyes, coins from different countries, saint medals, seeds, and so on. Many statues that come from Mexico even come already "loaded," meaning they have various items placed in the bottom of the statues sealed in resin. Many botanicas continue to make room for her products as demand increases.

A work station of the author, photo by Steven Bragg

Is La Santisima Muerte an Aztec Goddess?

Written in 2014

Many people claim that la Santisima Muerte is Aztec in origin, and they point to the popular Aztec goddess of death and the underworld, Mictecacihuatl. Although it can't be denied that Mictecacihuatl and la Santisima Muerte share some similarities—being represented as a skeleton or with a skull for a head and being a deity associated with death and the realm of the dead—these seem to be more superficial than at first glance. Recent evidence has come forward to question the common belief that la Santisima Muerte is the re-emergence of an Aztec goddess with a thin veneer of Catholic trappings.

In Andrew Chesnut's book, Devoted to Death: Santa Muerte the Skeleton Saint, in the chapter exploring Santa Muerte's history, he introduces us to La Parca, the Grim Reapress of Spain who, along with her male counterpart, the traditional European, bubonic plague-inspired Grim Reaper, carries the souls of the dead on to their next destination. The Black Death swept through Europe in the 14th century, leaving in its wake new manifestations of Death within the European mindsets, which may have still been fresh when Spain began its conquest of the Aztec Empire in 1519. Add to this that la Santa Muerte has been discovered in the Philippines, another area colonized by Spain, where effigies date back to at least to the 1850s, according to Chesnut's June 8, 2014, entry to the blog skeletonsaint.com. He further says, "This discovery, coupled with the existence of skeleton saints Rey Pascual in Guatemala and Chiapas and San La Muerte in Argentina and Paraguay, reinforces the indisputably strong Spanish influence in the origins of Santa Muerte in Mexico." So, it would seem that in many of the places Spain went and colonized, Catholic death saints and figures manifested or syncretized within the indigenous and folk populations.

Briefly looking below the surface at the Aztec claims, we can see that the Aztec Empire lasted less than two centuries before Spain arrived, and it only ruled a relatively small, southern portion of what is now Mexico. The better part of Mexico has been predominantly Catholic for over almost five centuries. In addition, Mictecacihuatl was only one goddess of several deities of death and the underworld. It's highly unlikely that one, singular goddess, who wasn't even honored for that long or by that many people, managed to survive underground and dodge the Inquisition in such a small area, and then later re-emerge throughout all of Mexico and parts of Central America. It is, however, more likely that the spiritual remnants of the Native underworld deities managed to latch onto the much larger personification of death brought over by the Spanish and survive, at least in the minds of the mestizo population.

Speaking of the Spanish Inquisition in Mexico, Chesnut shows us that in the Inquisitional records of the 1700s there is mention of localized devotion to "la Santa Muerte," specifically. Not Mictecacihuatl or any other pre-colonial name, but the Spanish name Santa Muerte. Although that's not definitive evidence, it does show that the religious and linguistic rule of the Spanish colonists had already heavily affected folk practices as early as the 1700s.

In his book, The Santisima Muerte: A Mexican Folk Saint, Bryant Holman recounts an interview with an informant who relays the story from Tehuantepec, Oaxaca, of the Santa Muerte of that region that rode "a cart creaking and straining as it was pulled down a cobblestone street." He points out the similarity to Don Sebastian of New Mexico who is a "skeleton driving an oxcart, which hauls the bodies of the dead away." Death driving a cart is an old tradition throughout European lore, and the squeaky axle reminds me specifically of L'Ankou of Brittany, who also drive a squeaky-axled cart to collect the souls of the dead.

Although I certainly do not discount the obvious effects the native, pre-colonial deities had on the development of la Santisima Muerte, as we see her today, it's becoming more and more clear to me that la Madrina has more European roots than was previously believed. As a European descendant, this makes a great deal of sense as to why la Muerte would have come to me so strongly, not that one has to be of European descent, of course, but everyone who can trace their blood back to Western Europe also traces their spiritual ancestry back to the Catholic Church and the veneration of the Saints, who in my opinion are elevated ancestors. The Church has always had a concept of the Angel of Death, through the Bible, and Europe is filled with older images and personifications of Death. It makes perfect sense that these images and forces came together with the native peoples in the New World (and the Philippines, it seems) to give rise to la Santisima Muerte.

What to Call Devotees and Workers of La Santa Muerte
Written 2014

Although there are no universally recognized "titles" for those who devote themselves to la Santisima Muerte, there are a couple of them that I've seen used. It should be noted, however, that these personal descriptors are not in any way a sign of an established priesthood or organization and can be used by anyone who has developed a strong connection to la Muerte.

Quick Spanish lesson for all of us Anglophones. "La Muerte" is the Spanish word for Death. Although it doesn't have the traditional "a" ending, it is a feminine word, denoted by "la". This may be a contributing factor as to why "Saint Death" has manifested in Mexico/Central America as female. One of many. Maybe, maybe not.

"Santa Muertero" for men, "Muertera" for women. Muertero/a is a Spanish word for someone who works very heavily with the dead, the muertos. (When you add "-ero/a" to the end of a word in Spanish, it's kinda like adding "-er/-ess" to the end of an English word, making it "someone who does this.") Now, add "Santa" to Muertero, and you have "someone who is devoted to/works with Holy Death. "Sta" is the abbreviation for "Santa," which I personally like because everyone in the English-speaking world thinks of Santa Claus when you write out Santa. Lol.

Another descriptor you'll see is "Santa Muertista" which usually only has the "a" ending. Personally, this seems like a borrowing from the term Espiritista as a general Spanish word for a person who works with spirits. Espiritista is used throughout the Spanish-speaking Caribbean islands (but is also found in Mexico, possibly due to the Cuban diaspora, which is also why you see Lukumi and Palo there) as one who is accomplished within the realm of Espiritismo, their version of Allan Kardec spiritism (which is a whole other ball of wax!)

So, Santa Muertero/a or Santa Muertista. Take your pick. And I'm sure there are probably others out there I've yet to encounter. La Santisima Muerte is very quickly growing, changing, expanding, and one never knows exactly what to expect from her.

Memorial altar for Santa Muertero Nick, photo by Steven Bragg

The Three Robes

La Blanca, The White

La Santisima Muerte of the White Robe, referred to simply as "La Blanca" is the eldest of the three traditional robes and is the first robe everyone should begin with. According to the Catholic mythos that's developed around her, in the beginning Death was not actively a part of the world. When Adam and Eve ate of the forbidden fruit (commonly thought to be the apple, which is why the apple is Santisima Muerte's most common offering), they were banished from the Garden of Eden, and they thereby brought Death into the world as an active force. Santisima Muerte manifested wearing a white robe.

La Blanca is concerned with the Natural order of things. Birth, Life, Death. Anything that interferes with this is something for which La Blanca may be petitioned. Disease can threaten or shorten a life, and so she can be called upon for healing. Witchcraft, hexes, and other sorcerous workings are the desires of people being forced upon others, causing the victims' lives to go in ways they otherwise wouldn't. Therefore, she can be called upon for cleansing and breaking curses. La Blanca can also be petitioned for guidance and wisdom, as she is the eldest of Elders.

Although all three robes should be approached as a Catholic saint would be, La Blanca is the robe that most insists on the respect due to a Saint and Archangel. Being the purest of the Trinity, she sits at the right hand of God. As the Holiest of Archangels, she can be seen with wings and the most powerful of the seven archangels (one for each day of the week). One should

22

refrain from using foul and sexual language in front of her, and, if possible, one should approach her in the state of physical and spiritual cleanliness. Prayers and requests should follow a Catholic form with regular mentioning that her power comes from God. She is the coolest and most merciful of the Three, although at times she can be stern and disapproving.

Sometimes it is said her true color is that of bone, because she is the death of old age, where one leaves behind a peaceful, complete set of bones. Because of this, La Blanca is also sometimes called La Huesa, or La Huesuda (The Boney One).

Her force is of a highly elevated nature, so if there are any dealings with La Negra, La Blanca and her elevated status must be respected by covering her statue with a white cloth. This is both respectful and practical for the worker, as it also shields her eyes from witnessing the workings that are not aligned with her nature. And because she sits at God's right hand, her statue must always be to the right of La Negra's, so the natural flow from the Divine is maintained.

La Blanca, photo by Mary D'Alba

La Roja, the Red

La Santisima Muerte of the Red Robe, referred to simply as "La Roja" is the second of the three traditional robes. Continuing the Catholic mythos, after Adam and Eve were banished from the Garden of Eden, Adam and Eve had sex, and from the blood that flowed from the death of Eve's virginity, Santisima Muerte took on the Red robe.

La Roja is a widely misunderstood robe in that most believe she is only for love, because it's generally thought that the color for love is red. That may be the case in many spiritual systems, however the reason Santisima dons the red robe in the tri-colored systems is because it's the color of blood, the living. La Roja deals with everything to do with worldly matters, and everyone in the living world has blood flowing through our veins. Therefore, sex, love, money, jobs, business, justice, government, the home, all of the things we deal with on a daily basis, fall within the working domain of La Roja.

La Roja is the first of the robes to make a more public appearance, dealing more with bringing back straying lovers. She does this not just because she's an expert on love magic, but because most of the time it's to re-unite the family for the sake of the home and children. She's a firm believer in staying true to your commitments and taking responsibility for your actions, which is why the scales are a major symbol for this robe. She will weigh your request against your own history, and decide if it's deserving according to the rules you, yourself, abide by and expect others to abide by, as well. She sees all that goes on in the world, so don't try to deceive her. She is the most accurate and final judge. She is equally skilled at manipulating court systems in favor of Her devotees.

The type of death associated with La Roja tends to involve a bodily fluid the same color as Her robe, including accidents, acts of violent passion, and death in childbirth. She would also be associated with miscarriages and the death of newborns and small children.

La Roja, photo by Mary D'Alba

La Negra, the Black

La Santisima Muerte of the Black Robe, referred to simply as "La Negra" is the third of the three traditional robes. According to the Catholic mythos that's developed around her, in the beginning Death was not actively a part of the world. When Adam and Eve ate of the forbidden fruit (commonly thought to be the apple, which is why the apple is Santisima Muerte's most common offering), they were banished from the Garden of Eden, and they thereby brought Death into the world as an active force. Santisima Muerte manifested wearing a white robe. When Adam and Eve had sex the blood that flowed from the death of Eve's virginity stained Santisima Muerte's robe red. After Cain slew Abel in the first act of murder, and the blood that fell to the ground and turned black, Santisima Muerte took on the Black robe.

La Negra is the hottest and most dangerous of the robes. She is the Death of sorcerous murder, violent murder, genocide, suicide, pestilence, and deaths that result from diseases of the mind. It is only when donning the black robe will Santisima venture into the depths of Hell to round up demons, along with her usual retinue of tortured and bloodthirsty souls, to do her bidding. Her children include diseases and plagues, and she can cause a person to become infected or increase the intensity of those who are already infected. In order to do healing work with La Negra, you must ask her to reign in her children and back off so La Blanca can come in and bring things back into balance.

Most go to La Negra for a variety of spells and protection from those same spells sent by others. She is a most skilled sorceress, equally capable of inflicting harm as well as shielding her children from it. Seated on a throne she becomes Queen of the Witches. This robe, more than the other two, should have an owl with her, as she more often turns the souls of witches who she worked for while alive into owls to work for her in death. *Las lechuzas.*

She is the least concerned with the human notion of ethics and morality, and more concerned with the well-being of those who serve her correctly. And this is where her negative reputation comes in, as La Negra is very often worked by criminals and the drug cartels, gaining her a great deal of negative media representation.

To work with her safely, however, the devotee must take regular cleansing baths to avoid the effects of her corrosive presence. Usually a bath of Holy Water, Siete Machos, rosemary, basil, rue, and salt will be sufficient.

La Negra, photo by Mary D'Alba

Lore and Guidelines

The Mysteries of the Flesh

It is said by some that Santisima Muerte's true form is not as a skeleton, but that she's actually a very beautiful, bloodless corpse with long, dark hair. However, because she sees us through the hourglass eyes of Death, she sees us as bones...what we eventually will be...and so she tries to relate to us in this way, showing us an image of herself in the way that she thinks we are. We see her as she sees us.

Muerte Encarnada is a skeleton only half covered with flesh, and some people use this image of her, while some have tried to make her more palatable to the public by using a fully fleshed statue of her...not very popular.

Making Peace with Death

Santisima Muerte comes for everyone, and making peace with that by working with her and knowing her will make the transition from life to death easier. Witches for whom she works while they are alive may be chosen to work for her after death as her "lechuzas" or owls.

Guadalupe, San Miguel, and other Saints

La Virgin de Guadalupe and San Miguel are the only other (official, Catholic) saints Santisima Muerte will tolerate near her. Keep other saints, especially San Cipriano, far from her altar.

Guadalupe can be seen in a few ways. Some say she is Santisima Muerte's sister; some say she is the light half and Santisima Muerte is the dark half. Some call Guadalupe the Mother of the Living, while Santisima Muerte is the Mother of the Dead. In any case, Guadalupe keeps Santisima Muerte in balance and can intercede for you if Santisima Muerte gets angry at you. You can have a small space for Guadalupe near Santisima Muerte's altar, including an image or statue, a candle, glass of water, flower vase, a rosary, and a small Mexican flag. Guadalupe's candle can be lit each time you pray to La Muerte, and a rosary can be said for her from time to time on Sundays and Mondays. Guadalupe's feast day is December 12, and you can set a table for her with a new candle, fresh roses, sweets, and so on and say a rosary for her.

San Miguel, Saint Michael the Archangel, protects, and he does so in a couple of ways. First, he's the most common saint to employ as one's amparo. Second, he protects Santisima Muerte's altars from spirits who pretend to be Santisima Muerte and who are attracted to her workings. He can be given a small space near Santisima Muerte's altar including an image or statue, a candle, glass of water, flower vase, and if possible, a sword or dagger. Light his candle each time you pray to La Muerte. St. Michael's feast day is September 29 and you can set a table for him with flowers, rum, Manischewitz, a cigar, and say a set of Catholic prayers for him.

General Guidelines

- Never ask another saint or spirit to do a work you already asked her to do. She is the ultimate force, after God, and it would be insulting to ask a lesser spiritual being to do something she has decided not to do. She should be a last resort if you work with other spiritual beings.

- If you've had sex, clean yourself before talking with La Blanca. Respect her sainthood, and if you have to have her altar in your bedroom, never have sex in view of her altar. Cover it or close it off somehow.
- Never threaten someone with Santisima Muerte, even idly or in jest. She decides what and when she'll do something. Period.
- Don't be (too) drunk when you're talking with her. She enjoys a drink, and she understands her children do too, however, approaching her should be done with control of mind and spirit.
- Never make a manda on someone else's behalf.
- Do not speak ill of the Dead, even if they were horrible people in life, they are with Santisima Muerte now and she looks after them.
- Always keep in mind that she holds the scales and anything you say will be weighed against the truth, so don't lie to her.

Preparing the Altar

The Altar

Santisima Muerte needs her own space, as she doesn't mix with other saints, spirits, or deities. It doesn't have to be large, just a clean space that's only for her. She prefers to be placed a little high up; do not place her on the floor. Do everything possible to make sure this altar is not in your bedroom or anywhere that she might see you naked. If you simply don't have space anywhere else, and it has to be in your bedroom, make sure it doesn't face your bed (and the various activities that may take place there). At the very least, cover her altar or make a curtain for her that you can close when you go to bed.

On the altar place an altar cloth of any color (white being a standard color to begin with), and on this place her statue, the clear glass of water, the central candle and the devotional candle, a plate for offerings, ashtray, and a flower vase. Guadalupe and St. Michael can be placed to the very extreme sides of Santisima, or if you only have the prayer cards or pictures, they can be mounted on the wall behind her. Arrange the altar so that Santisima is in the center and place everything else as you see fit or as she guides you. The altar can be shared by all three robes, as most people have limited space. It is not at all necessary to separate them.

Keep the altar clean. You can make cleaning her altar a weekly or monthly act of devotion. If you use an altar cloth, wash it along with this cleaning routine. Wipe down the surface with a mixture of water, Holy Water, and Siete Machos (or Rose Water). Food offerings should be removed as soon as they appear to go bad; do not let anything rot. Flowers should be taken off as soon as they begin to wilt. It's very important that fresh water always be present on her altar, so change it no less than once a week. If the water gets cloudy or murky sooner than one week, refresh it then, as La Santisima may be removing negativity from your life and placing it in the water. Therefore, never drink the water on her altar, and you can either pour it out outside or down a drain.

Statues

Properly blessed and charged statues are one of the most important aspects of honoring and working with La Flaca. They provide a physical vessel for her spirit so she can manifest in this world in the way needed to do work. The traditional working statues are between 9 and 16 inches in height with removable scythes. Honorary statues can be larger and of slightly more liberal decor and do not need to have removable scythes.

All statues should be "fed" by placing certain ingredients into the base of the statue and sealing it. These items include:
- raw rice (food for the statue),
- mustard seeds (used in her workings),
- a piece of red thread (to symbolize that she holds the thread between life and death),
- pinch of magnetic sand or a small magnet (for the power of attraction),
- coins (to always have money),
- charms or milagros (crucifixes, holy metals of her, St. Michael metals, etc.),
- her herbs,
- cemetery dirt, and

- powdered bone.

For La Blanca's statue add camphor to the above mixture. For La Roja's add cinnamon, and for La Negra's add patchouli and dried chili peppers.

If a statue doesn't already come with this in the bottom, or if it doesn't seem to have all these ingredients, then add a wooden base to the bottom of the statue with a hole in the middle. Place the statue on a piece of wood, draw the shape of the statue's base, and then cut along this line and cut a hole in the middle. Glue this base to the bottom of the statue, paint as appropriate, and fill the hole with the items and seal with wax. Do the last part in front of her altar as part of the baptism ceremony (after the copal smoke and before the baptism.) If you're not handy with wood, then at least make a small bag of white cloth to put everything into and tie to the statue so that the bag is hidden in the back.

An alternative to buying solid plaster (or whatever) statues are to make statues using a skeleton base. Either real (for the really big ones) or made from a material like wood or resin (for smaller work statues) they can be attached to stands and dressed appropriately and given all the appropriate objects (scales, globe, scythe, owl). The ingredients that would normally go in the bottom of the solid statues can be wrapped into cloth bags and placed inside the rib cage of this statue, creating a heart. For the work statues, again, make sure the scythes are removable and the hands don't grip them too tightly.

Once ready, the statue needs to be cleansed, fed, baptized, and dedicated to Santa Muerte. Pass it through copal incense smoke to cleanse it. Feed it as described above. To baptize the statue have a bowl of water and sprinkle Holy Water and Siete Machos in it. When ready lean the statue backwards over the bowl of water. Cup your hand in the bowl and pour the water over the forehead of the statue saying, "In the name of the Father," pour a second handful of water over the forehead saying, "in the name of the Son," and a third handful saying, "in the name of the Holy Spirit. Amen." Then blow cigar smoke all over it to bless it.

The Central Candle

A terra cotta or earthenware plate or saucer should be filled with dirts from the four corners and center of a cemetery, and a white candle should be placed in the middle. Always light this candle with a match and light all of Santisima Muerte's other candles from this one using those long fireplace matches. This is symbolic of Santisima Muerte's home in the physical realm being the cemetery, and by lighting all her candles from the central one, you are bringing light from the cemetery to her altar.

Central candle, photo by Mary D'Alba

Next, place a clean altar cloth over the surface. This can be the color of your strongest robe (white, red, or black) or use white if your main robe hasn't yet revealed herself to you yet. It can be plain or decorated with Catholic and/or skull imagery. It's up to you to be as simple or as creative as you want. If you put the spiritual cleansing mixture into a spray bottle, lightly spray the altar cloth. You can pray any prayers you want as you do this, or just talk to her either aloud or to yourself. Although she can certainly see what you're doing, it's nice to talk to her while you do it. Keep those lines of communication open as much as possible.

Arranging the Images/Statues

Now take your main image or statue of her and place it in the middle towards the back. Placing her in the middle show her respect and signifies that this space belongs to her. "Center stage" if you will. If you have more than one image/statue, place the others around the main one. And here's where some people get a bit confused, as it's easier to show this part than to explain it in writing. Look at the images of my altars to help. If you are working with her (or just praying to her) in the three-colored system I teach, and you have two or all three of the colors, who goes where is important. If you already know who your main robe it, place that one in the middle. If you don't know yet, place La Blanca, the white one, in the middle. If La Blanca is in the middle, place La Roja, the red, to the right, meaning YOUR right as you're looking at the altar. And place La Negra, the black, to the left. YOUR left. So, if you look at the altar as you're reading from left to right, it's going to be: La Negra (left), La Blanca (center), La Roja (right). If La Roja is your main robe, place her in the middle, La Blanca on the right, and La Negra on the left. So, from left to right it's: La Negra (left), La Roja (center), La Blanca (right). And if La Negra is your main robe, place her in the middle, with La Blanca on the right and La Roja on the left. So, from left to right it's: La Roja (left), La Negra (center), La Blanca (right).

The reason for these placements is because La Santisima Muerte sits "at the right hand of God" as the second most powerful force in the world. Meaning that if you were standing in front of "God" she's be to your left. So God's power flows from him to her (right to left), and La Negra, the least moral and least Catholic of the robes, can never be in between God and La Blanca, who is the purest of the robes and the eldest of the three sisters, and she must always be able to control the power of God so La Negra doesn't take it and try to upset the balance of powers. La Blanca is all about balance and the natural order of things. La Negra, if unchecked, can unleash rampant death and destruction.

Once you have your statues/images of La Muerte in place, then place your images/statues of Guadalupe and St. Michael on there. They go on the very left and right edges of the altar, or you can have small side tables or shelves. These two saints, or forces if you like, help keep things calmer and in check. Guadalupe can help keep La Muerte cool and understanding. St. Michael can help defend against trickster spirits and demons that may be attracted to your devotion or workings. You can use pictures, prayer cards, or statues, just make sure they're not larger than Santa Muerte's images/statues.

Placing the Altar Items

If you've made a central candle, where you've collected dirt from the four corners and center of a cemetery and place it in a terra cotta dish with a taper candle in the middle, then place this in front of the central statue of La Muerte, whoever is in the middle. This emphasizes your main robe. If you don't have a central candle as described above, then place your largest candle in front of the one in the middle. Place all other candles as you see fit. If you used candles of the three colors, then place those in front of their respective robes. Always keep fire safety in mind!

Next place the glass of water in the middle towards the front of the altar. I like to use a clear glass of water so I can see if bubbles or other signs appear. Keep this water refreshed at least once a week. Whenever I refresh her water, I usually either put three drops of Holy Water in it or I spray it lightly with the spray bottle. This blesses the water and signifies that it's for La Santisima. You can have glasses of water for Guadalupe and St. Michael, but that's not completely necessary.

Once the candles and water are in place, you can place all other items and offerings anywhere you'd like. Ashtrays, incense holders, offerings plates, flower vases, arrange all these in the way that is most pleasing to you. I like to keep a bottle of Holy Water on her altar. You can keep all of her spiritual water/cologne bottles on her altar along with any bottles of offerings. I use shot glasses to pour her a small amount of tequila or other liquid offerings at a time. When these start to go bad, pour it out, clean the shot glass, and pour another small amount. But keep the bottle closed so it lasts as long as possible.

As for the wall space behind her, decorate this as you'd like. I like to use Catholic imagery if I have the space, but whatever she moves you to do should be fine, keeping it within reason. If you've prepared an uprooted aloe plant (something I can talk more about in the future if there's interest), you can hang this on the wall behind her.

Final thoughts

Once all this is in place, you're fully set up to pray and work with her as often as you'd like. In the beginning, people love her so much they want to do things every single day. That's fine, at least start with, but over time it's inevitable that a person starts to feel a little burned out. Before you get to that point, have a talk with her and let her know that you still love her and will continue to pray to her, but set a realistic expectation that your life and schedule allows for. My current devotion to her is that I do a chaplet service for her at least once a month, but I try to light candles for her and refresh her water a couple times a week. If nothing else, each time I go into the room where she is, I cross myself, and say hello and give her thanks for all she's done for me. The beauty of folk Catholicism is that it's really just between you and the spiritual being you're working with or praying to. You make the connection, you keep the connection, and you work it out with that being.

That being said, remember to keep her altar clean, but you don't have to be obsessive about it. Sometimes I wait until just before one of her main feast days to do a full cleaning, taking everything off, washing the altar cloth, and wiping down her statues and everything on the altar. That's usually when I feel a surge of her presence and appreciation. But if I start to have strange dreams or just feel uneasy for more than a few days, I'll

42

go in and clean, refresh, and talk with her. Once I have her attention, that's usually when she lets me know if I need to do anything more.

La Blanca as main robe, photo by Steven Bragg

La Roja as main robe, photo by Steven Bragg

La Negra as main robe, photo by Steven Bragg

Offerings

La Santisima Muerte is a Holy Trinity, three persons in one. She is always Santisima Muerte, whether she is wearing the white, red, or black robe. However, when she puts on one of the robes, her personality shifts into the person of that robe. There are the usual offerings that can be given to her regardless of which robe she is wearing, and there are offerings that are given specifically to each of the Three.

Drink Offerings
- Water (tap or natural, but not bottled, and ALWAYS have water for her)
- Tequila, La Blanca prefers the light-colored tequila, and dark for La Roja and La Negra
- White wine for La Blanca, red for La Roja and Negra
- Sweet liqueurs for La Blanca, such as the clear Crème De Menthe, Aguardiente for La Roja, Whiskey for La Negra
- Coffee with white sugar for La Blanca, with brown sugar for La Roja, and no sugar for La Negra

Food Offerings
- Breads, tortillas
- Sweets
- Sugar skulls
- Fruit (especially apples)
- Honey
- Chocolate
- Dry white rice, can be mixed with dry white beans for La Blanca

- You can give two types of offerings of dry rice and beans for La Roja. One is white rice and red beans, and the other is brown rice with red beans. This shows how she stands between the workings of La Blanca and La Negra.
- Dry brown rice with dry black beans for La Negra

Smoke Offerings
- Cigars and cigarettes (blown directly onto her statue or image)
- Marijuana (blown directly onto her statue or image)
- White Copal Incense burned on charcoal
- Camphor and Rose stick incense for La Blanca
- Rose stick incense for La Roja
- Patchouli stick incense for La Negra

Perfumes
- Siete Machos (the main one you can't work without)
- Rose Water for La Blanca
- Florida Water and Bay Rum for La Roja
- Kananga water, Tobacco water, and Colonia 1600 for La Negra

Herbs
- Rosemary
- Basil
- Rue
- Mint, usually thought to be more for La Blanca
- Maguey Root (Agave), also called Century Plant
- Mexican Lovegrass
- Tobacco

- Marijuana
- Aloe
- Camphor, specifically for La Blanca
- Cinnamon, specifically for La Roja
- Patchouli and dried chili peppers, specifically for La Negra

Some of these can be offered as fresh bundles and hung on her altar to dry, and some can be placed dry in bowls and offered to her. Keep the tobacco and marijuana in glass jars with lids so she can keep an eye on them.

Objects and Other Offerings*
- Owl (should be with la Negra's statue if with no other)
- Money
- Scales
- Scythe
- Globe
- Rosaries (must be at least one on each statue and should be of same color as robe)
- Hourglass
- Flowers (especially roses but also carnations, however she'll accept any type of flowers)
- Clear quartz for La Blanca, rose quartz for La Roja, and smoky quartz for La Negra
- Make sure La Roja has money, a set of scales, and globe

*Always rub or sprinkle Siete Machos (that's had Holy Water added to it) on Santisima Muerte's objects and offerings.

The Devotional Rosary

The devotional rosary can be worn around your neck and used to recite the Chaplet for La Santisima. This rosary can be placed on the work table when doing specific work with her.

Cruz de Caravaca

The older and more traditional symbol is the Cruz de Caravaca. This is the cross that first arrived in what is now Mexico with the Spanish invaded and brought with them the Catholic Church. Some say that it's simply the Double Cross or Patriarchal Cross

An Amparo

La Santisima Muerte is one of the more recent manifestations of Death, and unlike other spiritual beings who may be from the Underworld, exert some control over the spirits of the dead, or who are guardians of the cemetery, Santisima brings with her an almost overwhelming energy that those who work with her frequently must be protected from. There is a traditional safeguard for this called the Amparo. The most common type of amparo calls upon St. Michael the Archangel, although a person could call on another saint that has military and protective characteristics, such as St. George or St. James.

To make an amparo with St. Michael, get two St. Michael prayer cards and place them back to back. Seal up the sides and bottom with tape, glue, or by sewing them, thereby making a small packet. Then go in front of a St. Michael image or statue and pray. Say 1 Our Father, 3 Hail Marys, 1 Glory Be, and say the St.

Michael prayer. Ask St. Michael to be your protection as you work with La Santisima Muerte. Write your name on a small piece of brown paper and place this inside the prayer card packet. Then place some hair from your head and some nail clippings inside. Drop a few drops of Holy Water inside and blow some cigar smoke into the packet. Seal up the top of the packet, closing it off completely, and baptize it in the name of the Father, the Son, and the Holy Spirit using Holy Water. Then place it between your hands and pray the St. Michael prayer over it. Offer St. Michael some cigar smoke and a strong spirit, such as rum or tequila. Close with 1 Our Father.

Keep this amparo under St. Michael's image or statue so he continues to protect you. Keep it hidden so no one else sees it. Every now and again bring it out and say the prayers again while holding it between your hands.

The Tribute

An important practice for La Santisima is La Tributa, the Tribute. The purpose of the tribute is to gain the attention of La Muerte for a specific purpose or working, as well as to provide her with an offering at the threshold of her home, the cemetery. This should be done when you begin with Santisima, especially if you wish to know if she will assist you in spiritual workings rather than simply accepting you as a devotee.

Obtain an unglazed earthenware vase or pot. If the only thing you can find is a planter, then seal the bottom drain hole as it needs to hold water. At least a day before you perform the ceremony of the tribute paint a white skull on the vase/pot and let it dry. You'll also need six white roses, seven dimes, water, Holy Water, and Siete Machos cologne. Remove any thorns and leaves from the roses.

When it's time, gather everything together in front of your Santisima altar. Say the opening prayers, including asking God's permission to call upon La Muerte. Talk to La Madrina as you place the roses into the vase/pot, add the water, add three drops of Holy Water ("In the name of the Father, the Son, and the Holy Spirit"), sprinkle in some Siete Machos, and add the seven dimes. When this is complete, tell Santisima that you are leaving to take her tributa to her home and to meet you there to receive it. Close with three Our Fathers, and then immediately take the tribute to a cemetery and place it in the gateway, neither completely inside the cemetery nor out of it. Talk to Santisima about the reason you're doing this, and when you're finished thank her, stand up, turn, and leave, but do not look back.

If you give her a tribute asking for her help, make sure that when she does it you give her a manda as payment, along with anything else you may have promised her.

The Manda

When Santisima Muerte has completed a work for you, you pay the Manda. You take the statue you worked with, place it on a small table in a fire-safe situation, and surround it with 12 candles, alternating the colors of 4 white, 4 red, and 4 black. Light the candles and let them burn down. Also, burn copal incense for her. Let the candles burn down completely and take any leftover wax to the cemetery.

The manda can also be in the form of an oil lamp. The following example contains rue, basil, camphor, and an olive oil base mixed with a Santisima Muerte oil blend, Siete Machos, Holy Water, and a Santisima Muerte medal. It has a floating wick, and it's in a special three-legged metal container available in many botanicas. It resembles a basic cauldron. You would allow this lamp to burn out on its own, as opposed to work lamps where you would keep refilling it for the needed number of days depending on the work.

Manda of candles, photo by Steven Bragg

Tattoos

Getting a tattoo of La Muerte is a common way of honoring her. It dedicates a part of your own body to her, however, should you ever renounce her and end your devotions and workings she may take that part of your body. The tattoo can be any image of her and where ever on your body you'd like to put it.

Skull Candles

One of the first innovations I was inspired to create with Santisima Muerte was the use of skull candles to make small focal points for her power. You take a regular skull candle you find in a botanica or online and carve a cavity in the back of the skull, leading all the way through to the eyes. Carve out the eyes and replace them with small mirrors, sealing the edges with wax. When hardened, you gather all the same items that go into a Santisima Muerte statue and go before her altar. Go through the same procedure of cleansing with copal smoke, placing the items into the cavity in the skull, sealing it with wax, baptizing, and blessing with cigar smoke. These can be placed on her altar to increase her power. They can also be placed around the room her altar is in and even high in the four corners of the room so they can keep an eye on things for Santisima Muerte.

Working with La Santisima Muerte

If Santisima Muerte chooses to work with you (as it is NOT the other way around), she will reveal herself beyond any doubt and usually in an impressively quick amount of time. The following information forms the basis within this system. Read through this thoroughly before attempting any workings with her.

Also, in my experience Santisima Muerte does not tend to mind photos of her altars being made public, however, I have been told not to make public photos of her workings. I can, on occasion, send a photo to a client who lives far away to show him/her the work has been done, but that is the only time I will take a photo of a working.

The Days of the Week

The days of the week can be used as a devotional guide for prayers, but it should be observed more strictly when preparing to do any workings.

- Monday: La Negra, good for protection.
- Tuesday: La Roja, good for justice and domination work.
- Wednesday: All Three, good to honor all three with the Chaplet service.
- Thursday: La Blanca, good for healing work.
- Friday: La Roja, good for love and money work.
- Saturday: La Negra, good for witchcraft.
- Sunday: La Blanca, good for cleansings.

Holidays

Two main holidays for Santisima Muerte are Good Friday and All Saints/Souls (Halloween, Dia de los Muertos). Good Friday is when Santisima Muerte was charged by God to reap his Son, Jesus, this being her highest honor it is the most important holiday. All Saints/Souls honors the rest of the cemetery and all the other souls she's taken on earth. For both holidays refresh the main altar and a table can be made in front of the altar and filled with flowers, candy, sweet confections, drinks, sugar skulls, etc. Mariachi music can be played. The Chaplet can be said. Family graves can be visited and cleaned up, leaving food and drink with them. Or, if away from family gravesites, you can tend a neglected grave and leave the food and drink there. A novena can be done prior to Good Friday, beginning so that Good Friday is the ninth day of the novena. An ad can be placed in the paper thanking Santisima Muerte for the year or a donation can be made to a charity in her name. For All Saint/Souls, say prayers for the dead and picnic in the cemetery, leaving lots of flowers and lighting red, white, and black candles.

Numbers

There is a system of numbers when working with Santisima Muerte. They are all odd numbers as odd numbers are believed to be stronger, while prime numbers are the strongest as they cannot be divided and therefore cannot be broken, and therefore the work cannot be broken. Santisima Muerte's numbers are 3, 5, 7, and 9, with 9 being more of a number of the dead in general. In workings the numbers are used in this way:

- 3 is for general workings,
- 5 is for opening up or fixing, also for protection,
- 7 is for drawing something to you,
- 9 is for dominating or mastering, and
- 13 is for uncrossing, reversing, and hexing.

La Dueña

The grave of "la dueña del campo santo" is the grave of the first woman buried in a cemetery and is where Santisima Muerte can be worked in any given cemetery. Offerings or working "leftovers" can be left at this grave, as well. However, if it is impossible to find the grave of la dueña, let Santisima Muerte guide you to the grave she wants to work at.

Petitions and Photos

The most common way of working with Santisima Muerte is by writing a petition, or taking a photo of someone and writing the petition on the back, and wrapping it around the scythe at the point where the hand holds it and "placing it all in her hands." Before this, however, the petition and/or photo needs to be baptized with Holy Water and anointed with Siete Machos along with whatever oils and/or powders. Then smoke it, breathe on it, and quickly pass it through a candle flame. Petitions and photos can also be placed or stuffed elsewhere on her statue, where ever there is room. When Santisima Muerte has completed the work, or made known she isn't going to do it, remove the petition and/or photo and take it to the cemetery. Personally, I make it a rule not to read petitions placed with Santisima Muerte by others. For those petitions I've prepared small wooden boxes that I place them in after a certain amount of time, three months or so.

The Hourglass of La Blanca

The hourglass represents the finite amount of time you have in this life before Santisima Muerte comes for you. Working with the hourglass brings this in. For a healing, working with La Blanca, you can start the hourglass and just when it's about to empty flip it, then wait until it's halfway and lay it on its side. Ask Santisima for just a little more time for you or the person you're working for.

An Apple Working

Bore a hole down the center of an apple and place a candle in it. Place the petition and some herbs inside the apple, then place the candle (red, black, or white) in the hole. Drizzle this with honey and place it on a plate, surrounding the apple working with sacred herbs. Light the candle, pray over it, and place this at Santisima Muerte's feet. This can be repeated for any sacred number of nights (3, 5, 7, 9, 13) with a new apple, petition, and taper for each night. When finished all leftover items should be taken to the cemetery.

Influencing the Person's Spirit

To help a working that influences a specific person, you place the photo and/or name paper under a clear glass of water, the water providing a channel to the person's spirit.

Fasting

You can fast during a work, usually 3 days, but it can be done for 7 or 9 days (for a novena), too. No food from sun up to sun down.

Oil for La Blanca

Using a base of Olive oil, add either vitamin E or jojoba oil as preservatives. Add to this dried herbs of Rosemary, Basil, Rue, Mint, Maguey Root, Camphor, and White Copal. White rose petals can be used as a substitute for one of the herbs. Add a few drops of Holy Water and Siete Machos. Use this as the base oil for working with La Blanca.

Oil for La Roja

Using a base of Olive oil, add either vitamin E or jojoba oil as preservatives. Add to this dried herbs of Rosemary, Basil, Rue, Maguey Root, Cinnamon, and powdered Dragon's Blood. Red rose petals can be used as a substitute for one of the herbs. Add a few drops of Holy Water and Siete Machos. Use this as the base oil for working with La Roja.

Oil for La Negra

Using a base of Olive oil, add either vitamin E or jojoba oil as preservatives. Add to this dried herbs of Rosemary, Basil, Rue, Maguey Root, Patchouli, Dried Chili Peppers, and Yellow Mustard Seed. Add a few drops of Holy Water and Siete Machos. Use this as the base oil for working with La Negra.

than an inch tall to avoid soot from staining the walls of the room.

Gather up the following items: Lamp container, terra cotta saucer, wick, cigar, dried herbs, brown piece of paper about 2 x 2 inches, 6 needles, Santisima Muerte oil, olive oil (large amount), Siete Machos, and Holy Water.

Say the opening prayers and explain to La Muerte what you're doing and ask for her assistance in the matter. Write your petition on the piece of brown paper and sign it. Baptize it with the Holy Water and Siete Machos, blow cigar smoke on it, breathe on it, and quickly pass it through a candle flame. Then take the 6 needles and make 3 crosses in the petition by weaving them in and out, crossing two at the time. After making the first cross say, "In the name of the Father," after the second say, "in the name of the Son," and after the third say, "in the name of the Holy Spirit. Amen." Place this in the bottom of the lamp container. Sprinkle the dried herbs in the container, and fill it (to about half an inch below the top of the container) with the olive oil. Add the Santisima Muerte oil. Place the wick on the top of the oil, give it some time for the cotton to absorb the oil, and dip your forefinger and thumb into the oil and saturate the top of the wick. The lamp is constructed. Now baptize it with the Holy Water and Siete Machos and bless it with cigar smoke. Light the wick from the central candle on Santisima Muerte's altar, and carefully hold the lamp up to the four directions. Pray to the Santisima Muerte, explaining that this lamp is going to remain lit for however many days it needs to be, and the remains will be taken to the cemetery. And promise her a manda if she does this for you. Pray hard and put a lot of emotion into your prayers.

Each day refill the lamp with the olive oil. If the flame goes out, simply re-light it from the central candle. Once the lamp is done, place all the leftover remains into a small plastic bag, and place this into a brown paper bag with 7 dimes. Take this to the cemetery and bury it at a grave (la dueña's grave or another.)

Lamp working, photo by Nick Arnoldi

Prayers

The following sets of prayers are a combination of traditional Catholic prayers, folk prayers, and recently created or altered prayers to the used for la Santisima Muerte. Many of these prayers were received from Nicholas Arnoldi in 2011.

Opening a devotional or working session includes the Persinada, the Our Father, Hail Mary (three times), Glory Be, St. Michael Prayer, and the Evocational Prayer. Ending a session consists of saying a protection request and the Our Father three times.

Opening and Ending Prayers
As Received from N. Arnoldi in 2011

The Persinada

To be done upon approaching her altar, or working her, or when you feel danger or bad vibes. Hold your thumb up and the index finger bent to form a cross, and the three remaining fingers standing straight up to represent the three nails of the crucifixion.

Through the sign of the cross (make the sign of the cross between your eyes),
From our enemies (make the sign of the cross over your lips),
Free us, Oh Lord (make the sign of the cross over your heart),
Through the intercession of the Santisima Muerte.
In the name of the Father, the Son, and the Holy Spirit.
Amen.

Our Father

Our Father, who art in Heaven, hallowed be thy name. Thy kingdom come, Thy will be done, on earth as it is in heaven. Give us this day our daily bread, and forgive us our trespasses, as we forgive those who trespass against us. And lead us not into temptation, but deliver us from evil. Amen.

Hail Mary (X3)

Hail Mary, full of grace, the Lord is with thee. Blessed art thou among women and blessed is the fruit of thy womb, Jesus. Holy Mary, Mother of God pray for us sinners, now and at the hour of death. Amen.

Glory Be

Glory be to the Father, to the Son, and to the Holy Spirit, as it was in the beginning, is now, and ever shall be, world without end. Amen.

St. Michael

St. Michael, the Archangel, defend us in our day of battle. Be our safeguard against the wickedness and snares of the Devil. May God rebuke him, we humbly pray, and do thou, O Prince of the Heavenly Host, by the power of God, thrust into Hell Satan and the other evil spirits who prowl through the world seeking the ruin of souls. Amen.

Evocational Prayer

Almighty God, before your Divine Presence, (sign of the cross) *in the name of the Father, Son, and Holy*

Spirit, I ask permission to invoke the Santisima Muerte.
Holy and Powerful Mother, at this moment I beg for
your presence and intervention. Through the great
power, which God has given you, I beg of you to hear
my prayers and grant me all the favors I ask of you
until the last day, hour, and moment when the Divine
Majesty shall call me before his presence. Santisima
Muerte, beloved of my heart, do not abandon me
without your protection. (Sign of the cross) *In the name*
of the Father, the Son , and the Holy Spirit. Amen.

Now speak to her as you need to, say her Chaplet for
her, or do whatever workings needed.

Ending Prayers

In the name of the Father, the Son, and the Holy Spirit.

Santisima Muerte, Our Most Holy Mother, I beseech
you lovingly to protect those who carry your prayers
and devoutly honor you. Cover them with your mantle,
and guard them with your scythe, that their enemies
may not have dominion over them. Protect them from
bad luck, disease, and envy; witchcraft, hexes, and
curses; lightning, fires, and earthquakes; demons, evil
spirits, and phantoms; evil eyes, evil hearts, and evil
minds; cover them, oh Holy Mother, so that no evil can
see them, no evil can touch them, and no evil can follow
them. In the name of the Father, the Son, and the Holy
Spirit. Amen.

Our Father (X3)

Our Father, who art in Heaven, hallowed be thy name.
Thy kingdom come, Thy will be done, on earth as it is in
heaven. Give us this day our daily bread, and forgive us

our trespasses, as we forgive those who trespass against us. And lead us not into temptation, but deliver us from evil. Amen.

A La Blanca altar of the author, photo by Steven Bragg

Devotional Prayers for the Three Robes

Composed in 2012

Prayer for La Blanca

Santisima Muerte, La Blanca, Most Holy Death of the White Robe, eldest of the Three, you who sit at the right hand of God, hear our prayers. Glorious Huesuda, you who grant the peaceful death of old age and heal the sick, through the great power, which God has given you, we ask you to remove all sickness from our lives. Niña Blanca, with your holy scales, bring balance to our bodies, minds, and souls and protect us from all illness. Santisima Muerte La Blanca, Holiest of Archangels, cover us with your pure robe, we pray. In the name of the Father, the Son, and the Holy Spirit. Amen.

Prayer for La Roja

Santisima Muerte, La Roja, Most Holy Death of the Red Robe, born from the first love, hear our prayers. Niña Roja, you whose powers over matters of the heart are beyond compare, know our desires and grant us what we ask. Glorious Madrina, you who work within the world, through the great power, which God has given you, we ask that you assist us with our many needs. Santisima Muerte La Roja, Holiest of Archangels, protect us from the deaths of your robe. In the name of the Father, the Son, and the Holy Spirit. Amen.

Prayer for La Negra

*Santisima Muerte, La Negra, Most Holy Death of the
Black Robe, born from the first murder, you who are
the hottest of the Three, hear our prayers. Powerful
Muerte, enthroned as queen of the witches, only you
can descend into Hell and not be touched by the
demons and spirits that reside there. Fearsome Mother,
you grant the strongest protection from curses,
witchcraft, and evil spirits, and the diseases of the
world are also your children, who you send and take
way at will. Grant us your protection, La Negra, and
cover us with your shadowy robe. This we ask in the
name of the Father, the Son, and the Holy Spirit. Amen.*

Photo by Mary D'Alba

70

The Fifth Mystery: the Hour Glass – our time on this earth is ticking away every second. Each passing moment brings us closer to our death.

(Next Bead)
Our Father, who art in Heaven, hallowed be Thy name. Thy kingdom come, Thy will be done, on earth as it is in heaven. Give us this day our daily bread, and forgive us our trespasses, as we forgive those who trespass against us. And lead us not into temptation, but deliver us from evil. Amen.

(Next 10 Beads)
Santisima Muerte, beloved of our hearts, do not abandon us without your protection, defend us from our enemies, and grant us a peaceful death. Oh, Holy Mother, hear our prayers. Amen.

(Then recite)
Glory be to the Father, to the Son, and to the Holy Spirit, as it was in the beginning, is now, and ever shall be, world without end. Amen.

(Closing prayer)
Oh, Glorious Santisima Muerte, we beseech you lovingly, that with the great power which God has given you, that you remove all darkness and evil from our lives. Protect our homes and our loved ones, and fill our lives with the grace of your presence. Santisima Muerte, beloved of our hearts, do not abandon us without your protection. Amen.

(Holding the Cross or Medal)
Through the sign of the cross (make the sign of the cross between your eyes),

From our enemies (make the sign of the cross over your lips),
Free us, Oh Lord (make the sign of the cross over your heart),
Through the intercession of the Santisima Muerte.
In the name of the Father, the Son, and the Holy Spirit.
Amen.
(Kiss the cross or medal.)

Finally, say the Ending Prayers.

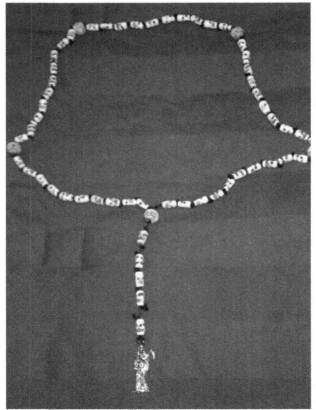

Santa Muerte Rosary, photo by Steven Bragg

Various Prayers, Invocations, and Novenas
As Received from N. Arnoldi in 2011

Jaculatoria

Muerte, dear to my heart, do not abandon me without protection, without your protection and for me do not leave (name of person) one moment of tranquility; bother him every moment, mortify him/her and disturb him/her so that s/he always thinks of me.

Praise Prayer

You are, O, Muerte, immortal because you have conquered the world, overcoming difficulties with your profound knowledge. O, Santa Muerte most sacred, Make it so that I always triumph in the world of grief and agony, and the peace you give a dying man in his last agony as you take him from the world. O, Most Sacred Muerte, Make it so that I always triumph in the world for the pains one feels from your emanation, when the coldest of your followers begin to feel emotion. O, celestial Death, make it so that I always triumph in the world. O, celestial Death make it so I always triumph in the world. O, celestial death, already soothing my grief, unite me with the ones that have passed, whom I loved so much. O, celestial Death, make it so I always triumph in the world. It will be a great pleasure and a proud moment to join the First. By your will, O, sacred Muerte, make it so I always triumph in the world. By our Lord Jesus Christ. Amen.

Prayer to Attract the Spirit of the Person

Spirit, body, and soul of (person's name); *come because I summon and dominate you; tranquility you cannot have until you come surrendered at my feet. Just as I past this needle through the middle of this candle, thus shall thoughts of me will pass through the middle of your heart so that you may forget the wo/man you have and come when I call you* (Repeats this 3 times)
Angel of your day, angel of today, Guardian Angel of (name of person), *bend the heart of* (name of person) *so that s/he/they may forget the wo/man/person s/he/they has and come surrendered of love unto my feet.*

Prayer to call the Guardian Angel of the person

Holy Guardian Angel of (name of person), *may you not allow him/her tranquility until he be by my side. Saint, oh Saint of my name and devotion that I took affection and desire of San Salvador de Orta, that s/he be content with me is what matters to me. Anima Sola de Juan Minero, that s/he may love, that I may love him/her. Santa Ines del Monte Perdido, return to me the affection of (name of person) who has gone.*

Spirit, body, and soul of (name of person); *that from this moment s/he/they may not have any joy, any desire other than that for me; Spirit, body, and soul of* (name of person) *that his/her/their love, his/her affection, his/her fortune, his/her/their caresses, his/her/their kisses, everything of him/her/their be only for me. Body and soul of* (name of person) *you may not go to see nor love any other wo/man/person than me.*
Spirit of San Cipriano, bring him/her/them here to me, Spirit of Santa Elena, bring him/her/them to me, Spirit of Santa Marta, bring him/her/them to me, Spirit of La

Caridad del Cobre, bring him/her/them to me, Virgen de Covadonga, that you might bring me (name of person.) (One repeats this three times. Having now named the spirit, one says:) *Spirit of the light that illuminates the clouds of the souls, light the brain of* (name of person) *so that s/he/they remembers me and all that s/he/they has you may give me, impulse through your powers so that s/he/they may be a slave to my love; tranquility do not give him/her until s/he/they may be at my side. Amen.*

Prayer to the Aloe

Virtuous Aloe, Blessed Aloe, Holy Aloe, Sacred Aloe; through your virtue that you gave to the Apostles I ask that you extend to me this virtue because I venerate you and I love you, so that you may free me from Evil Acts, Sickness, Bad Luck, that my businesses and business transactions do well; that you drive away evil from my home, and that you free me from enemies everywhere I may go: that you may give me work, Blessings, Fortune and Money with all ease and the least effort, your virtue will make me strong, famous, fortunate and joyous, do not place obstacles in all that I am ambitious for, desire or propose to do, make for me a flattering success; this Divine Virtue that God gave you, in God I believe and in you I trust. Through all of the virtues that you concede to me I will defeat all of the obstacles that are presented to me and my home will fill with blessings with your virtue sublime and portentous Holy Aloe. Amen.

Prayer for Health

Santisima Muerte, you have the power to heal all illnesses, or inflict them. I come before you, begging for your assistance. You know the cure for all sickness, and can administer it to free men from their suffering. Oh, Holy Mother, I beg you to have compassion on me (or whom you are praying for) and grant them a miracle, for the pains that they suffer. Amen.

Prayer for Good Luck

Santisima Muerte, you travel all roads, and know the paths of fortune. With your cloak, cover me, to shield me from evil, and lead me down the path of good luck, so that I may receive all the blessings if your holy protection. May everything I do in business be prosperous, May all my finances grow, May all good luck come to me, through the glory of your powerful intercession. Amen.

Prayer for Business

Immaculate and Powerful Santisima Muerte, who gives the power to obtain our desires, allow my business to succeed. Give me the tranquility and security to allow my business to prosper with abundance, and let it always carry your blessings. Allow for the money to bring me satisfaction and multiply it for my benefit, and the benefit of my love ones. Amen.

Prayer for Money

Oh, Holy Mother la Muerte, in your hands all things shall come to dust. No gold or silver can turn your gaze, nor block your path. You cast it aside as dust, just as you will do to our flesh when the Divine Majesty calls. Oh, Holy Mother, place me in the path of gold, Oh Holy Mother, place me in the path of silver. Let prosperity come to me, but assist me to always

remember that one cannot serve God and Mammon,
and wealth is only a useful tool, when one does not
become its slave. Amen.

Prayer for Employment

Santisima Muerte, you know what lies down all paths,
and can see beyond all roads. Lead me down a
prosperous path, that I may find employment that will
be befitting the vocation which the Divine Majesty has
ordained for me. Assist me in this necessity, for in God
I believe, and in you I confide. Amen.

Prayer for Protection

Santisima Muerte, hold me in your powerful arms, and
shadow me with your mantle. Protect me from all harm,
let no evil befall me.
To those who wish me harm:
Blind their eyes, so they can't see me
Bind their arms, so they can't grab me
Bind their feet, so they can't follow me
Stop their ears, so they can't hear me,
and Cloud their minds so they'll forget me.
Amen.

Prayer of the Blades

(Razor blades or knifes – to be placed over doors and
windows for protection)
Compassionate Lady, shed your light in the dark places
for your devoted servant, so that your loved ones shall
be kept away from ill wills. With your power, make the
light return after the darkness, and bless these places,
so they may cut through the bad airs before they enter,
and stab at any evil intruders, as well as keep the forces

of the elements at bay. Bless these blades, so they may break through negative intentions, and fill my home with the joyful blessings of your protection. Amen.

Prayer to Stop Slander

Oh, Glorious Mother, Santisima Muerte, intercede for me now on my behalf. Into your hands, I place the image of the one who speaks evil tongues against me. Oh, Sacred Angel, sew shut their mouth; and cut their tongues, so they may never again speak evil of me. Should their thoughts turn against me as well, I beg of you to hold their breath in your powerful hand, that they cannot speak their wickedness. Amen.

Prayer Against Enemies
(The Prayer of the Scythe)

Santisima Muerte, la Negra, I come before you, kneeling at your feet, imploring your force, power, and omnipresence against those who intend to destroy me. My Mother, I ask that you be my shield and protection against the evil my enemies may send against me. With your scythe, cut through all obstacles that they have placed in my way, and open all doors they have closed to me. Clear my path, and lift me up beyond their reach, that their wickedness may not touch me. Amen

Prayer to Remove Evil

Oh Santisima Muerte, Our Blessed Lady of the Land of the Shades, I beseech your presence and intervention. With your cloak, cover me with the mantle of your holy protection, and with your scythe, cut down all evil that presents itself in my life, my home, my job, and my way. With your great power, which God has given you, I ask that you banish all evil spirits, evil spells, witchcraft, hexes, curses, evil eyes, evil minds, and evil hearts from my presence. My most Holy Mother, look through the darkness that surrounds me, and remove all these evils. Amen.

The "Red" Prayer "Oracion de la Santa Muerte"

Jesus Christ the Conqueror, who on the Cross was conquered, conquer (name of person), *that s/he/they be conquered for me in the name of the Lord. If you are a fierce animal, be tamed as a lamb, tame as the flower of rosemary; you must come. You ate bread, of Him you gave me and through the most strong word that you gave me, I want you to bring* (name of person), *that s/he/they be humbled and defeated at my feet, to complete what to me s/he/they has offered. Santisima Muerte, I beseech you lovingly inasmuch as Immortal God has formed you with your great power over all mortals so that you might place them in the Celestial Sphere where they may enjoy a glorious day without night for all eternity and in the name of the Father, the Son, and the Holy Spirit, I pray and beseech you that you deign to be my protectress and that you concede all the favors that I ask of you until the last day, hour, and moment in which your Divine Majesty commands to take me before your presence. Amen.*

Novena for Love
(Recite the Jaculatoria before each day)

First Day
Santisima Muerte: The favors that you grant me will defeat all difficulties and nothing will be impossible for me. No insurmountable obstacles, enemies, or people who wish me harm will defeat me. May everyone be my friend, and may I dominate any business or anything I set out to do. May my home be filled with the good virtue of your protection.

Second Day
Santisima Muerte, my great treasure, do not leave me on any occasion: You ate bread and of him you gave me and as the powerful owner of the Dark Mansion of Life, and the Empress of the Darkness, I beseech the favor that (name of person) *presents him/her/theirself at my feet humiliated and repentant and that never again shall s/he/they leave my side, as long as I may need him/her/them. And make him complete that which he has promised to me.*

Third Day
Jesus Christ the Conqueror, who on the Cross was conquered, conquer (name of person), *that s/he/they be conquered for me in the name of the Lord. If you are a fierce animal, be tame as a lamb, tame as the flower of rosemary. Adored Muerte, I supplicate you affectionately that with this titanic strength which God gave you, that you place me inside the heart of* (name of person) *so that s/he/they only has eyes for me and that I am everything for him/her/them, and I will light a candle every Tuesday for you each week at twelve midnight.*

84

Fourth Day

Dearest Muerte: I ask of you with all the strength of my heart, that as God formed you immortal and powerful Mistress and Queen of the Darkness of the Beyond, that with the great power that you have over mortals, that you make it so that (name of person) *cannot eat at a table, nor sit in a chair, nor have any tranquility. I desire that you oblige him/her that, humbled and defeated, s/he/they comes to my feet and never may leave me again.*

Fifth Day

Glorious and Powerful Muerte, taking advantage of your generosity, as my protectress and mistress, I ask you this favor, as the invincible lady that you are, I beg you that you see that (name of person) *cannot enjoy going out, that s/he/they cannot go out with wo/men/people, nor eat nor sleep if s/he/they is not at my side, that his/her thoughts be only for me, and the same for his/her will and that s/he/they gives me all the happiness of all of his/her/their love.*

Sixth Day

O Sovereign Lady! To whom the Divine Trinity of the Eternal God placed for reaping the lives of all mortals, to whom all arrive either late or early and to whom riches or youth matter not; You who are the same with the old, the young, or with children, to those that you should take into your domain when God so indicates. Oh, Sovereign Lady! I supplicate thee that (name of person) *falls very much in love with me, that s/he/they does not fixate in physical beauty, but rather in that of my soul and that s/he comes to me submissive, loyal, and kneeling at my feet.*

Seventh Day

Immortal Muerte: Free me from all evil and with the titanic power that you have, which God has gifted you, see to it that we enjoy an eternity of glorious days without night. For this, my protectress and mistress, I ask that you concede to me these favors that I ask in this novena. (make petition)

Eighth Day

Miraculous and Majestic Muerte: I ask of your immense power, that you return to me the affections of (name of person); *that you leave him/her/them not one calm moment, not may s/he/they be at peace with wo/men. If s/he/they is sleeping, may s/he/they dream of me. If s/he/they is awake, may his/her/their thoughts be only of me and the words I speak to you, may you hear them and do as I ask of you.*

Ninth Day

Blessed Protector Muerte: Through the virtue that God gave to you, I ask that you free me from all evil designs, dangers and illnesses, and instead you give me: luck, Health, Happiness and Prosperity. May you give me friends and free me from my enemies, and make it so (name of person) *presents him/her/themself before me humble, to ask pardon of me, humble as a lamb, and loyal to his/her/their promises, always loving and submissive*

Novena for Any Petition

First Day

Santisima Muerte, before your Divine Presence I kneel, begging a miracle from your hands, to alleviate my suffering. The Holy Trinity has formed you with Great Power; You who transverse all roads and pathways, who knows what men hold in their hearts, I beg of you, hear my prayer and answer me. (Mention your petition.)

Second Day

Santisima Muerte, beloved of my heart, do not abandon me without your protection. Oh, Holy and Immaculate Being of Light, I beg of thee to look with compassion upon me and my petition. (Mention your petition.) *Oh, Holy Angel of God, who shall come to each and every one one of us, who has the power to remove the soul from the flesh, I beg of thee to grant the petition I place before thee.*

Third Day

Santisima Muerte, God has given you to us as a most powerful intercessor in times of need. Have pity on me, though I am unworthy of it; and look with compassion upon my offering of tears, which I lay at the foot of your throne, confident in your protection and intercession. (Mention your petition.)

Fourth Day

Santisima Muerte, confident in your compassion for all beings, I come before you pleading for your intercession in my time of need. You who can travel the world in the blink of an eye, let my prayer be heard just as quickly, and on your swift wings, give me a sign of your assistance. (Mention petition.)

Fifth Day

Santisima Muerte, with open arms I welcome you into my life and home, assured that your Holy Presence will be a shadow of protection and grace upon me and those I love. Oh, my saving angel, I beg of thee and thy power, grant this prayer I ask of you. (Mention your petition.)

Sixth Day

Santisima Muerte, with your cloak you cover your children with the shadow of your protection, and with your scythe you ward off all evil. Most gracious Mother! Behold me kneeling at your feet, pleading with you for this grace. (Mention your petition.)

Seventh Day

Santisima Muerte, you can alleviate my suffering, for the Divine Majesty has filled you with power. Confident in your compassion for your children, I come before you, and ask that my prayer be heard. (Mention your petition.)

Eighth Day

Santisima Muerte, your very name strikes fear in the heart of evil spirits, and even angels fall from their stations when you spread your glorious wings. With such power and majesty that you possess, I beg that you will use your Divine force to answer my prayers. (Mention your petition.)

Ninth Day

Santisima Muerte, I am confident that you will answer all prayers laid at your holy feet, and in thanks for the many blessings you will bestow upon me, I promise to love and honor you always. Stretch for your hand for me, and let my prayer be granted. (Mention your petition.)

Invocational Prayer

(This prayer is to be said in an ecstatic fashion.)

Santisima Muerte, Santisima Muerte, Santisima Muerte, we ask that you come to us and for the joy we feel when you are with us, mi Niña Blanca, mi Rosa Maravilloso, lead us on every path and protect us from all evil.

Santisima Muerte, Santisima Muerte, Santisima Muerte, we pray to you, Our Lady, to venerate you, let us feel you, and fill us with joy because you are with us, and you give us your protection. And we are not afraid because of all the virtues you possess. We will overcome all obstacles, Santisima Muerte of our heart. Do not forsake us and give us your protection.

Santisima Muerte, COME! We ask this with all our heart, gracias, gracias, gracias, for being with us and in the name of the Almighty God the Father, we offer and recite the following novena prayers. (Say prayers.)

Gracias, mi Niña Blanca, gracias, mi Rosa Maravilloso, for staying with us, blessed be! Thank you for listening to us and we thank you for the protection you provide us and we ask that you come to us each and every time you are invoked, or whenever one of us needs you.

Gracias, mi Niña Blanca, for all you give us. Be blessed, Santisima Muerte, thank you for giving us this time of joy.

Gracias, Santisima Muerte,
Gracias, mi Rosa Maravilloso,
Gracias, mi Niña Blanca.

Prayers for the Week

Monday
Santa Muerte, I ask you to start this week with blessings to my family, my home, and my work. Protect me from all evil. So be it. Amen.

Tuesday
Niña Blanca, at your feet I bow and I urge you to give me health. Send away any illness so that I make move forward. I ask you this with all my heart. Amen.

Wednesday
This day I will not ask for anything, but if you appreciate me, offer your protection to both me and my loved ones. Continue to cover them under your mantle. Amen.

Thursday
Today, before leaving, I ask you to open all roads that will lead me to a tranquil life. I do not ask for luxuries, just that you give me enough to live without worries. My faith is placed in you. Amen.

Friday
Hermana Blanca, I pray that the owl that always accompanies you will give me the wisdom to know how to guide my family to always know how to act as good people. I trust in you. Amen.

Saturday

Mi Flaquita, thank you for letting me see the light of day again. As thanks, I promise to think of you, and I offer you this prayer for my requests to be heard. (Say petition.) *Thank you for everything you have given me. My trust is in you. Amen.*

Sunday

Thank you Santisima Muerte, for being near me these seven days of the week. Thank you for giving your protection to me and my home and removing all evil that surrounds us. My devotion is yours forever. Amen.

Photo by Mary D'Alba

The Ancestors
Written between 2002 and 2018

From my point of view the foundation for everything
spiritual we do begins with our ancestors, those who
came before, paving the way, continuing their traditions
(or creating new ones,) and continuing the bloodlines.
Whether intentionally or not, their efforts have
preserved the lines of communication between the
physical and the spiritual. Those of us who actively
work with our ancestors generally don't refer to it as
ancestor "worship," but ancestor veneration. We honor
them, remember them, and in many cases provide them
with simple offerings to keep them close to us in
exchange for their protection and wisdom. In many
systems, such as the African Diasporic Religions
(ADRs) the ancestors are so important that no
ceremony can be done without first giving honor to
them. In these systems it's possible for a person's
ancestors to block all communication with any other
spiritual beings until they are given their proper service.

I teach that there are generally three types of ancestors:
ancestors by blood, ancestors by adoption, and
ancestors by initiation. Everyone has the first type,
many people have the second type somewhere back in
their ancestry, and some people will gain the third type
after they initiate into a traditional spiritual system.
Ancestors by blood are the strongest ancestors a person
will have. Blood is spiritually and magically one of the
most powerful substances, as it carries the very essence
of life, and a blood connection to something or
someone is one of the strongest connections. It is also
because of the blood connection that we can speak
directly with our ancestors without asking permission
or help from a gatekeeper, such as Legba or Elegua.

Blood ancestors have an invested interest to help their descendants carry on the bloodlines and maintain their honorings. Ancestors by adoption can work more in the manner of a clan or tribe. And ancestors by initiation have a contractual obligation to help the initiate. The line between adoption and initiation ancestors many times blur as the nature and functions of the two can go hand in hand.

In traditional societies, a person only venerates ancestors in his or her direct blood lineage. So, father/mother, grandfathers/grandmothers, great-grandfathers/great-grandmothers, and so on. Aunts, uncles, cousins, etc. aren't normally included. This is because it's presumed that everyone is being honored by their direct descendants. However, in today's Western society, ancestor veneration has unfortunately been lost by most people for many centuries. Because of this, I find it very appropriate to include in a person's service any family member, and even any close friend or friend of the family, who has passed on, especially if that person happens to appear in a dream or spiritual reading or service.

Over the years, I've been asked about not having a good relationship with family members and whether or not that affects a person's service. What everyone needs to remember is that every single person has literally countless ancestors stretching back to the dawn of humankind. We're only ever going to have personally known the tiniest fraction of our ancestors. That being said, ancestors that far back have most certainly already been completely re-absorbed into the spiritual infinite, or, as they say in some societies, they have joined the stars and watch over us from the night sky. However, we still have access to hundreds of ancestors, many of whom will have no problem stepping forward to help us. They can block any troublesome family members and, if possible, facilitate reconciliation and healing, if that is desired by the person. Simply talking about this to your ancestors can have a large impact on your service and connection to them.

Whether our ancestors were Jewish, Christian, Muslim, Pagan, or whatever when they were
alive, there are many ways to venerate and work with them all. In many of the Spanish-speaking Caribbean and South American countries, the Allan Kardec-based "Espiritismo" systems are used to work with a wide variety of spiritual beings, including ancestors. *The Ancestor Novena*, the ceremony to help establish a connection and service to a person's ancestors that I've recommended for many years, comes from Espiritismo, however, there are many, many variations of this that are just as effective. If you join a traditional system, of course, follow the advice from your elders. Always remember, though, that your ancestors are YOURS, and no one else's. Once you've established that connection and you feel confident the lines of communication are strong and consistent through the test of time, follow their guidance and advice on how best to serve them.

(The following ritual was originally written and published on Witchvox.com in 2002. I've made a few alterations to it over the years.)

The Ancestor Novena

This ritual, although seemingly simple, has enormous effect on a person in that If a person has never successfully established contact with one's ancestors, this will allow for the ancestors to come fully into the person's life.

In the beginning you should only establish contact with direct blood relatives, meaning parents, grandparents, great-grandparents, and so on. In an ideal ancestor-venerating society, all other relatives, such as aunts and uncles, would be taken care of by their descendants. However, in the majority of the Western world this is sadly not the case. In some cases, passed extended family members may have had a greater effect on you than your parents, and those spirits may wish to be honored in your line of ancestors. This is fine; however, they should be invited into your ancestral honorings after the direct blood relatives. Those extended family members and even the spirits of those not related to you by blood can be included in your service to your ancestors after this novena has been successfully completed by calling their names, maybe placing a picture of them on the altar, and asking them to join your ancestors during one of your regular services. In the case of adoptions, you have two sets of ancestors, and they can be served all together.

Items to obtain for the novena:

- One or two white 7-day candles (large, tall candles encased in glass), or a set of white tapers
- Cascarilla or white chalk
- A clear glass of water
- Perfume or incense of a soft, light nature (with an incense holder)
- A corner of your home or small space that's not in your bedroom which can be used to house your ancestors.

Items to have for the ninth day:

- A white plate
- White flowers
- Food that they may have enjoyed in life, cooked by you, with no salt added (if the ingredients inherently contain salt, don't worry about it, but do not ADD salt). Salt drives away the dead.

Preparation

Clean the space you have chosen for your ancestors. If you plan to have an altar table, that's fine, but during the novena place everything directly on the floor. If you have pets partition this area off somehow so they will not have access to it. Take the cascarilla (or chalk) and draw an arc on the floor from one wall to the one perpendicular to it. If for some reason, you can't use a corner but a section of wall instead, make this a half-circle, starting from one side of the area, moving around it, and closing it in on the other. The purpose is to spiritually close off this section. Using the cascarilla (or chalk), make nine short dashes along the arc or half-circle. It should look like railroad markings on a map. Place one 7-day white candle or taper inside the marked-off area, along with the clear glass filled with water. Place the bottle of perfume or the incense inside the area. Choose a certain time of the day that you are sure you can be free to talk with your ancestors at the same time for nine consecutive days, beginning on a Monday.

The Novena

When the time comes settle yourself in front of the
area, light the candle, and open the bottle of perfume or
light the incense. Prepare yourself for spiritual
communication. I suggest saying one Our Father, three
Hail Mary's, one Glory Be, and a pray to St. Michael.
Ask God's permission to invoke the Santisima Muerte,
say a prayer to her, and then ask her to help you
establish communication with your ancestors. Then
state your full name and call to your ancestors. The way
I like to do it is to say,

*Ancestors by blood, ancestors by adoption, and
ancestors by initiation; ancestors I know and ancestors
I don't know; I thank you for everything, because
without you I wouldn't be here. If I stand tall in this life
it's because I stand on your shoulders.*

Do this at the beginning of each session. Then just talk
with them the way you would family members at a
family reunion, catching those up who have missed the
latest bit of your life, and introducing yourself to those
you never met. Tell them what you're doing (the
novena) and why it's important. Ask them to come into
your life and help you do what you need to do. When
you've said all you wish to say, thank them again. If
you wish to sit and spend time in their presence that's
fine, but after that tell them you will be back again at
the same time and place to talk with them more the
following day. Finish the session with asking them to
always bless, guide, and protect you.

Extinguish the candle or allow it to burn the remainder
of the day/night until you go to sleep, or allow the

candle to burn continuously throughout the novena, which will require at least two 7-day candles.

On the Ninth Day

Do your prayers as usual, talk with your ancestors, and then explain that this is the last day of the novena, and that from now on you will come to them once a week to light their candle, supply fresh water, and talk with them. At this time you can place the altar in the area and place all their items on the altar (this is "lifting them up"), give them the flowers you've gathered or bought, give them the food you've prepared, and thank them again for being a part of your life.

After the Novena

Monday is the most common day to honor your ancestors. Light their candle, give them fresh water, give them food if you feel they need it and whatever type they ask for (again with no salt added), give them flowers, alcohol, cigarettes, whatever they enjoyed in life, and talk with them. Place pictures of them and items they owned on the altar. Remember that once you've given something, such as a bottle of rum or pack of cigarettes, it belongs to them and isn't for personal use.

While chatting with them share with them your good news and bad news. When you feel you need help in life's journey, ask them for support and wisdom. Once you have established a good relationship with your ancestors, let this relationship evolve as they guide you. In other words, this is only the beginning.

A Few Cemetery Guidelines
Written in 2013

The following is general information that I've received over the years throughout my training in the various traditions I hold. None of it will be specific to any tradition, therefore none of it will be "secrets" I'm giving out. These concepts and tips are commonly found within many of the Afro-Caribbean and New World living folk traditions, although the spirits and details vary from tradition to tradition. If you've been initiated and/or trained in tradition that employs the cemetery, then stick with what you were taught. This is more for those who are starting out or those who haven't yet received the spiritual license and protection many of the initiations of these traditions provide. Also, just because these are general tips from different traditions, please don't try to use them to create your own hodge-podge practice. For example, don't use this information to petition Oya at the gate of the cemetery, so you can walk up to the central cross to honor Baron Samdi, then proceed to a grave calling on Exus and Pomba Giras to team up with Santisima Muerte to help you kill someone. Please don't try that. Instead, you can use what you find here for simple honoring of the dead, collecting cemetery dirt, when you need to take something to the cemetery for Santisima Muerte, and to generally protect yourself when you feel like taking an afternoon stroll through the domain of the dead.

Denizens of the Cemetery

To give you an idea as to what you need protection from, let's look at who and what can be found in and around the cemetery. First and foremost, there is the cemetery gatekeeper. This is the spiritual being who controls the flow in and out of the cemetery for many spirits and who should always be recognized and paid by a living person before entering. Failure to do so can result in the gatekeeper allowing nasty spirits to leave the cemetery with you and follow you home to cause trouble. Don't snub the gatekeeper, as he/she performs a vital role in keeping young and confused spirits from wandering out of the cemetery and moving in with you! If you're part of a tradition already, you're going to work with your tradition's gatekeeper. If not, don't worry, just keep it simple and respectful, and devotees of Santisima Muerte can call on her to intercede on their behalf.

By far the majority of the spirits encountered within the cemetery walls are the ones you would expect, the dead. Not all the dead buried here will be present, but a lot of them will be. Who are these folks? Well, they're people, like you and me, just without bodies or a sense of linear time/space. Some may be confused, sad, angry, desperate, whatever. The spirits of those who haven't moved on to where ever it is they go or haven't accepted they're dead will be the ones encountered easily and randomly. Their spirits many times linger near their body, whether they know it or not. If you happen to get the attention of these spirits the results can vary. They may try to take their anger out on you, or try to get your attention to help them, or follow you home to be near someone.

Just above the general dead in risk level are the spirits who realize they're dead and have over time began to learn how to use this to their advantage. They've started to figure out how things work and how to get what they need from the living. Again, these can be the spirits of many types of people, including drug addicts, alcoholics, and murderers. They can from time to time leave the cemetery after the sun sets, with the permission of the gatekeeper, but usually they have to return by morning, unless they can find a person or place that they can latch onto. A person walking home drunk in the middle of the night tends to be a favorite.

Beyond those just mentioned, the more advanced and elevated spirits of the dead have a higher potential for being dangerous. Typically, they're much older and have been around the block quite a few times, and by a few times I mean centuries. They can also leave their own cemetery and go into others with little trouble. Some of them may have been spiritual workers in life and decided to stay around the physical realm to continue working for people in exchange for payment(s). Lacking a strict set of ethics, they must abide by, they can be very tricky and typically have their own interests at heart. Tricksters are among these spirits, the ones who can pretend to be higher spirits, deities, and even sometimes try to imitate Santisima Muerte in order to receive service from people.

Further up the hierarchy we encounter those who rule over the cemetery, and generally the threat level goes down for most living people, especially those who have not been initiated into any specific priesthood or magical order. These spiritual beings heed little attention to the majority of the living. It's the priests and sorcerers who have to deal with them to grant permission for any major workings to be done in their domain. However, an untrained, uninitiated person dabbling around the cemetery without showing proper respect is likely to attract some attention from these beings, with the possibility of them sending some of the more dangerous spirits home with that person to teach some harsh lessons.

The last spirits I feel I need to mention are the ones that really should be a concern to most people, experienced or novice. These are dark, twisted spirits of that are full of and induce anger, hate, malice, obsession, addiction, and more. Spirits, some of which were once people and some that never were, who for whatever reason have been transformed into something far from human and closely resemble what most people in the Western world would consider a demon. They can be found dwelling in an abandoned crypt in the cemetery or lurking in shadows outside the walls. These spirits rarely seek out living victims on their own, but they can be sent by some of the more advanced ones to do whatever work needs to be done. Regardless, it's best to always be protected when going anywhere these spirits might be.

Cemetery Precautions and Guidelines

Before you even leave your house to go to the cemetery, you should exercise caution by covering your head. The head is the seat of the soul, in many spiritual systems, and covering it while in the cemetery is one of the easiest, yet most important, things you can do to protect yourself. (As a side note, this can also be applied anytime you go somewhere that more than likely can be a source of negative spirits and influences, such as a hospital, bar, or jailhouse, or when you journey out at night.) You can wear a hat, baseball cap, head wrap, bandana, whatever. If you want to make it a little stronger, sprinkle a few drops of holy water inside the hat or cap or on the cloth before putting it on. Wear whatever protective jewelry, including scapulars, holy medals, or whatever else you may have. Place in your pockets whatever protective objects you have made or had made for you. It wouldn't hurt to have a small bag of salt on you, as well. If you have any open wounds, bandage and cover them. Finally, make sure you have pennies or some other coins to use as simple payment for entry into the cemetery and to leave as offerings or payment for whatever you're doing.

When you approach the cemetery gate (or where the gate should be), pause and knock three times. Announce who you are (you don't have to do it out loud) to the gatekeeper and ask permission to enter. Drop three coins and walk in (the number of coins in addition to offerings vary from tradition to tradition, but for something simple, three is a good number.) Some people walk in backwards to prevent being identified, but for simple visits this isn't really a concern. If you're just there to walk around or visit a loved one's grave, you've pretty much done all you need to do. Just be respectful while you're there. Don't speak ill of the dead, and act as if you're in someone else's home—because you are.

If you've come to leave offerings or deposit a working (be careful with this until you have more experience and training from an experienced teacher/godparent under your belt!), find the location you're looking for, leave the offerings or work, leave the payment, take three steps backwards, turn, and walk away without looking back. And as you leave the cemetery it might be a good idea to take out that little bag of salt and throw some behind you over your shoulder after you've gone a few steps through the gate. You may also want to take a cleansing bath when you get home—it helps if you've already made it beforehand and it's ready the moment you arrive. Also, in these cases it would help to have a line of salt placed across the threshold of your door before you leave. (If you haven't noticed by now, salt is very effective in protecting against many spirits of the dead, the less elevated ones, that is.) These last few steps of should also be done if you've decided to go and clean up some gravesites, as some people like to do around All Souls Day. It's not always a great idea to go home and relax covered in cemetery dirt.

Going to the cemetery at night is when extra precautions should be taken, and this really shouldn't be done by a novice or untrained person. Nighttime is when many spirits of the dead are more active, along with the others discussed earlier. Those tips I just mentioned should be done anytime you decide to visit the boneyard after the sun sets. Be careful and listen to your instincts. If you get an uneasy feeling while there, just leave. Again, I stress finding a competent teacher or godparent to guide you before doing anything in the cemetery after dark.

The signs that you've picked up something from the cemetery or something's followed you home can vary greatly. However, they usually include restlessness, paranoia, difficulty sleeping, unpleasant dreams, lack of energy, sudden illness, unusual mood swings, among other unpleasantries. If you experience a combination of these symptoms after doing anything in a cemetery, seek out a competent person who can determine what the problem is and provide a solution. A cleansing of your body, along with your home, will take care of most problems, but if you're not experienced, I highly suggest finding someone who can do this for you. Most likely they will charge you, because it is time and work, along with exposing themselves to the problem, but most of the time it's well worth it.

The outdoor shrine of the New Orleans Chapel, circa 2012, photo by Steven Bragg

Origin of the New Orleans Chapel of the Santisima Muerte
Written in 2014

The New Orleans Chapel of the Santisima Muerte owes its existence to the teachings of Nick Arnoldi, aka Hechicero Nick. A New Jersey native, Nick spent a year in Mexico in 2001 and met an hechicero (native sorcerer) who was known as Don Gilberto within his community. When someone was born with a special gift to work within the spiritual realm for the benefit of the community he was said to have the "don." Don Gilberto passed Nick the system of working with La Muerte which consisted of the three robes of white, red, and black. Nick returned to NJ and maintained his personal connection to la Flaka, working for clients over the years. Nick and I met in MA in 2008, but it wasn't until after I returned to New Orleans that the subject of the Santa Muerte came up. Before returning she had approached me in a dream and offered a solution to a problem I was having. At that point, not having any experience with her, I was hesitant, but I accepted. She fulfilled her end of the bargain, and I repaid her as best I could. She remained content with this until about a year later when she made it known she wanted me to work with her more. I set the condition that she needed to bring me a teacher before I'd go further with her, and right after is when Nick brought his devotion and workings with her. A couple of days later Nick contacted me saying La Muerte came to him in a dream and instructed him to teach me and pass along Don Gilberto's system.

La Muerte wasted no time in responding to my prayers through this system, and she quickly became the dominant spiritual force in my life and practices. Once I got to a comfortable point with her, I asked for a major, personal favor. Within a couple of weeks she delivered what I asked for, and I knew then that this relationship was the one I'd been preparing for most of my life. So, in payment I built an outdoor shrine as my way of spreading her devotion. Around the same time, the indoor space I had set up for her grew exponentially, and she eventually took over an entire room in my home. This became the indoor, private chapel. Before I could even put on the finishing touches, Santisima began to bring other people to attend the chaplet services I hold for her, and in two and a half years there is now a very close-knit family of devotees and beginning workers who live in New Orleans and other places. We've been honored to have as guests other traditional workers of La Muerte, as well as Prof. Andrew Chesnut, the leading academic of Santa Muerte in the English-speaking world.

Tragically, Nick's life ended soon after my training in his system was completed. It seemed Santisima Muerte wanted him to pass along his teachings before she came for him. He has an altar in the chapel, and I make certain to keep his memory alive and spirit honored. Without him, none of this would have been possible. I've been blessed to have some of his friends in New Jersey contact me and send me many of his statues and devotional items to continue their service in the New Orleans Chapel. His best friend, Lorraine, who knew Nick since high school and remembers when he was in Mexico has visited, and we've exchanged stories of Nick's personal and spiritual life.

Liturgical Calendar
for the New Orleans Chapel of the
Santisima Muerte
Written in 2017

When I received my information about la Santisima Muerte it included two main feast days and a system of honoring the three robes throughout the seven days of the week. These were, of course, loosely based on the Roman Catholic liturgical calendar and syncretic folk devotional/magical practices. The first of La Flaka's feasts is Good Friday, I was told, as it was La Muerte's highest honor for God himself to ask her to reap his only Son. The second feast time is the three-day death-oriented period of Halloween, All Saints Day, and All Souls Day. The days of the week are divided between the robes with La Blanca having Sunday and Thursday, La Roja having Tuesday and Friday, La Negra Monday and Saturday, and Wednesday shared by all three. Those familiar with Western occult systems will see somewhat obvious planetary correspondences at work.

I realize many people outside of Santisima's Central American lands of origin, particularly English-speaking folks, don't feel the need to maintain her Catholic roots, which is completely up to the individual. Those familiar with my work, however, know that I do, and there are three main reasons for this. The first reason is because this is how I first encountered her, and I'm a bit of a traditionalist. Secondly, she came to me in a dream and told me she wanted me to maintain this way of working with her. This should've been the end of it right then, but a third reason has recently manifested as a result of the five years since founding the New Orleans Chapel and holding regular chaplet services. That reason is the City of New Orleans and my personal connection to it.

New Orleans is historically a Catholic city, and the Archdiocese here is the second oldest in the United States. Catholic churches, shrines, and cemeteries abound here. Streets are named after saints, and Catholic festivals inundate secular life, including most notably the Mardi Gras, St. Patrick, and St. Joseph celebrations. Like in many of the Latin and Caribbean regions of South and Central America where Catholicism accidentally became fertile ground, or at least a mask, for unique religious diversity, such as the Afro-Diasporic Religions and unrecognized folk saints, New Orleans has its own flavor of home-grown spiritual practices that have sprout up over time, unlike much of the surrounding Protestant-dominated regions in the rest of the Southern U.S. Therefore, it should come as no surprise that in just a few years La Muerte, the mestiza folk saint of Mexico, has quickly taken root here and is beginning to flourish.

Although I was raised in a Pentecostal Protestant church, I adopted some folk Catholic practices and observances after moving to New Orleans in 2001. The history and pageantry were too tempting to pass up despite my affiliations with modern paganism and Wicca. At about the same time Haitian Vodou and ancestral veneration made their way into my spiritual life, setting the stage for the Santisima Muerte to step out of the shadows and steal the spotlight after my 2010 return from my four and a half year hurricane-induced exile to Massachusetts. Since then, and since my initiations into other Afro-Diasporic traditions, New World ways of doing things have outstretched my pagan practices with a recent upswing in the folk

Catholic side. I don't consider myself to be Catholic, even though I have been baptized, but I've experienced stronger and faster results in my spiritual world when I tap into the dominant spiritual influences that surround me. In my opinion, Saints (and saints) are elevated ancestors (and spirits,) "Marys" are broadly speaking manifestations of the Mother of God, and using the trappings of the Catholic Church, such as rosaries and holy water, is a respectful way of gaining their attention and sympathies. This is obviously oversimplified, but suffice it to say I don't need to buy into the official theology behind it all, as it simply works for me.

During a quiet point in the Mardi Gras celebrations that just ended I was sitting with La Muerte, thanking her for all she's done and thinking about an upcoming chaplet service when it occurred to me how very "La Negra" the season of Lent is, especially considering the end of it with Good Friday and Holy Saturday being big nights for those who work with the black robe. Then La Roja got my attention to observe how very "La Roja" the season of Carnival is. And it just went from there! Just as the seven days of the week are ruled over by the three robes, there could also be seven seasons of the year where one robe (or all three) takes dominance. So, the following is what I've worked out after some consideration of the Catholic cycle of the year, and the New Orleans Chapel will begin incorporating these observances in its liturgical calendar. I'll most likely be expanding this into its own booklet, including rituals and services as I write them and see how they work in practice.

Part of the year will be "fixed" meaning there will be specific dates every year, while part will be "mutable" as these dates change each year depending on when

Easter falls. It has a very syncretic feel, which is in line with La Santisima's nature as I've come to know her. Also, I should note that although I'm drawing from general Catholic holidays and seasons, I'm not too interested in sticking to any specific interpretations behind them other than the most obvious and commonly held ideas.

1. Advent and Christmastide: La Blanca
   - Fixed: Immaculate Conception, December 8 through January 5

As Mary (actually Guadalupe, whose feast day is conveniently December 12) is the mother of the living and La Madrina is the mother of the dead, many say they are sisters, and so it stands to reason in my opinion to follow the Catholic observances of Mary in relation to Santa Muerte. Also, since La Muerte was such an important part of the story of Mary's son Jesus (he had to die for it all the work,) why not begin with the anticipation of his birth, Advent. This through Christmastide is a very sacred time as the savior of the world is born and is announced in the heavens with the Star leading the Three Magi to Bethlehem. Sacred and celestial are the realms of La Blanca, the white robe, the eldest and purest of the three.

2. Carnival: La Roja
   - Fixed/Mutable: Epiphany, January 6 through Mardi Gras

Referred to as Ordinary Time in most other places, here in New Orleans Epiphany on January 6 begins the season of Carnival. And it's all about the indulgences! Food, booze, and sex reign supreme, and these most certainly fall within the terrestrial realm of La Roja, she of the red robe. The festivities, balls, and parades continue until Fat Tuesday, where they reach an astounding climax. *insert wink here*

3. Lent: La Negra
- Mutable: Ash Wednesday through Holy Saturday

With the passions of the red robe behind us, we move towards another Passion, the Crucifixion and death of Christ. Before this, however, is Lent, the solemn time of reflection and for many here recovery and regret. (This might even appear in the form of some of the black robe's children: STDs. Give it a couple weeks, but go to a clinic and get tested.) La Negra has come through for me as the most stern of the three robes, the least comforting, and the most frightening. The violence Christ suffered of a drawn-out, agonizing murder sits squarely in her realm, as do the fires of Hell to which he descended. After Jesus' death and descent, the brujos go to work. While the Christian world is dark and devoid of its God, those who deal in sorcery and witchcraft have free reign. Good Friday and Holy Saturday are better spent staying indoors and behind the protection of the blessed palms gathered the Sunday prior.

4. Eastertide: La Blanca
- Mutable: Easter through Pentecost

Making it safely through Lent and Holy Week, we find that Christ returns resurrected and Death dons her most brilliant robe once again. The Church celebrates God on Earth before he ascends to Heaven. La Muerte happily celebrates her role well done. This continues through when Christ ascends until the Day of Pentecost, sometimes called White Sunday, when the Holy Spirit descends upon the disciples. The celestial elements of La Blanca are obvious.

5. Midyear: All Three Robes
   • Mutable/Fixed: Pentecost through August 14

Now comes another period of Ordinary Time and summer, a time in today's world when many people vacation and travel. With most divine beings in heaven, the living roaming the earth, and hell safely where it should be, all three robes are in their respective domains and can be celebrated as desired.

6. Harvest: La Roja
   • Fixed: Assumption, August 15 through September 30

Many already celebrate August 15 as a feast day for Santisima Muerte, perhaps due to the afore-mentioned connections between Mary and La Muerte, so observing this is already commonly known. Although not part of the Catholic calendar per se, it shouldn't be missed that the end of summer is the time when many things are harvested from the earth and just a few centuries ago many more people where focused on gathering the fruits of the land and culling their herds in preparation for winter. This traditionally European time of reaping and bloodshed, terrestrial toiling, falls within the ruler ship of La Roja. Her robe isn't red because of love, but because of the blood that came forth from the death of Eve's virginity after she and Adam were expelled from the Garden of Eden.

7. All Hallows: La Negra
   • Fixed: October 1 through December 7

Finally, we come to the time of year when many think of death, ghosts, ghouls, and witches (in the U.S., at least.) These days Dia de los Muertos decorations can be seen everywhere during this time, and a blending of more U.S./European Halloween and the Catholic All Saints and All Souls is occurring in some areas. Quite clearly this would be a time to celebrate La Negra and those who return from the Underworld to visit the living. La Negra's protection is much appreciated while this is happening.

This is the basic idea of the new liturgical calendar I intend to adopt for the New Orleans Chapel. Things may change and will hopefully develop over time. If this speaks to you, I happily invite you to try it for yourself and let me know how it works out. The only thing certain in life is Death (and taxes), and the only thing certain with how she is being honored is if it has any effect for those doing it. Best wishes!

Photo by Steven Bragg

In Loving Memory
Of Nicholas Arnoldi

April 29, 1984 – August 6, 2012

Made in the USA
Monee, IL
05 January 2022

88037054R00069